THE BRITISH SOLDIER IN THE 20TH CENTURY

Written and illustrated by

MIKE CHAPPELL

WESSEX MILITARY PUBLISHING

ed taylor 20/7/24 chase militaria

Published in 1989 by
Wessex Military Publishing
P.O. Box 19
Okehampton, Devon EX20 3NQ
© Copyright 1989 Wessex
Military Publishing

ISBN 1 870498 08 9

Typeset and printed in Great Britain by
Toptown Printers Limited
Vicarage Lawn, Barnstaple, North Devon
England

Photographic processing by C.J.P. Photographic

The Vickers replaced the Maxim .303 inch machine gun in British service.
Seen above is the Maxim section (then of only one gun) of the 1/5th
Prince of Wales's Own (West Yorkshire Regiment), early 1900s. Below is
the Maxim section of the 1st King's Royal Rifles, Chitral, 1895. Note the
early-pattern mount, a fore-runner of the Mk IV. (Malcom Carr and the
National Army Museum.)

The Vickers Mk I 1914-18. Above, a M.G.C. officer checks a gun that has lost its muzzle attachment. Right, a Vickers of the 20th (Light) Division on its "emergency" mount supports the French 22nd Division near Nesle, 25th March 1918. Below, M.G.C. men replace water evaporated from the barrel casing of their gun, 1917. (Author's collection.)

COLOUR PLATE A

Within a machine gun company of the Great War period, a six-man detachment "crewed" a Vickers Mark I machine gun. Each was allocated a number. The "number 1" fired the gun and was assisted by the "number 2". "Numbers 3 and 4" were ammunition carriers, "number 5" a scout and "number 6" the range taker. (Two such detachments formed a sub-section under a Sergeant and a Corporal; two sub-sections a section, and four sections a company.)

Weapons and ammunition were carried into action from the "fighting limbers", the No. 1 carrying the tripod and the No. 2 the gun. The central figure depicts a Lance-Corporal No. 1 of 'D' company, 37th battalion M.G. Corps on the Western Front in 1918 and demonstrates the way the tripod was carried. (Note the battle insignia of our subject's unit, the pistol carried as a personal weapon, the No. 8 belt box and the spare parts case which should have been carried by the No. 4, but was usually retained by the No. 1.) The Mark IV tripod in its original form is shown in the photograph at top, left. Below this a 1944-vintage photograph shows a No. 1 setting up the tripod in position. Comparison of the tripods will show the improved direction dial introduced c.1915 at the same time as graduated elevating wheels.

Once the tripod was in position the No. 2 brought up the gun and helped the No. 1 to mount it, whilst the Nos. 3 and 4 brought up ammunition and the condenser equipment. The gun was now ready to be loaded, aimed and fired in response to the fire control orders issued by the Section or Company commander.

In May 1918 a Guards Machine Gun Regiment was formed, consisting of four battalions, the 4th (Foot Guards) battalion supported the Guards Division, whilst the 1st, 2nd and 3rd, all formed from the Household Cavalry, were under command of the First Army. The figure at left demonstrates the insignia worn by the "Machine Gun Guards" of the Guards Division prior to May 1918.

An interesting item of uniform worn by machine gunners in 1915/16 was the "waistcoat" shown at right. The heavily padded shoulders were designed to prevent burns from hot barrel casings. The garment was frequently worn by No. 1s to prevent galling from the 48-pound tripod. It was soon discovered that sandbags gave just as much padding as the "waistcoat" which was rarely seen after 1916. Note the rolled P.H. gas helmet and the insignia of the 53rd M.G. Company, 1915.

Other insignia shown includes the crossed-Vickers cap badge of the Machine Gun Corps, range-finders (R) and machine-gunners (M.G.) skill-at-arms badges, and the shoulder-titles of the Machine Gun Corps' infantry (I) and cavalry (C) branches.

COLOUR PLATE B

A *"Motor Machine Gun Service"* of the *Royal Field Artillery was formed in November 1914 and absorbed by the Machine Gun Corps in 1915. Sections and batteries of the "M.M.G.s", as they were called, were afforded extra mobility by means of their motorcycle combinations — the standard model being the Vickers-Clyno illustrated, 1918. The Vickers machine gun could be mounted to fire forward of the sidecar, or to its rear — as shown.*

The central figure is that of a Sergeant of the M.M.G.s, and he wears the breeches and leather gaiters adopted as most suitable for motor-cycling. His gauntlets and goggles are also motor-cyclist's items. For foul weather the M.M.G.s were issued with waterproof jackets and trousers, but our subject makes do with a standard leather jerkin. Note his pistol, and the binocular case, compass case and map case vital to a machine gun fire controller. His insignia includes a M.M.G. cap badge "sweated" to his steel helmet, "Motor Machine Guns" titles, and "M.G." skill-at-arms badges worn above his badges of rank to show M.G. instructor status. A "small box" respirator and a machine gun clearing/cleaning rod complete his outfit. At his feet are 500 rounds of belted ammunition in two "Boxes, belt, Vickers .303 inch M.G., (metal) No. 8".

To the right rear strides the figure of a M.G.C. Major, 1917. His brassard and insignia mark him out to be the divisional machine gun officer of the 50th (Northumbrian) Division — a Territorial Force first-line formation serving on the Western Front.

Insignia illustrated includes the cap badge and metal shoulder title of the M.M.G.s, the skull-and-crossbones set on the silhouette of the M.G.C. badge adopted by the 117th M.G. Company, the M.G. over III of the 3rd (Guards) M.G. Company and the M.G. on a blue diamond of "C" Company, 42nd battalion M.G. Corps. One of the most original devices was that of the 101st M.G. Coy. It showed a green "fuzee with chain" on a dark blue ground. The fuzee converted the tension of the fuzee spring into rotary energy to power the Vickers lock on its forward, firing action. It could be said to be the heart of the gun.

The photograph at top, right shows a machine gun section of the 12th M.G. Coy, 4th Division, at Arras in 1916. No. 1s and No. 2s are armed with pistols and they wear a red-on-khaki device on their sleeves. (Reproduced below.)

Below, right is a portrait of a Lieutenant of the M.G. Corps (ex-13 King's, Liverpool) on occupation duties with the 3rd Division in Cologne, 1919. Note the buttons of the Kings, the collar badges of the M.G. Corps and the divisional sign of the 3rd Division — shown in detail above. (Paul Reed and author's collection.)

Over its half-century of service
a variety of vehicles, most of w
left, the 3rd Special Reserv
transport one Maxim and one
quickly replaced by the "Wago
Here, eight vehicles haul the 1
1916. Note that the off-horses
at left — 1 Welch, North-West
Vickers were carried in "15-
manufacture. Those at right
Northumberland Fusilier M.G.

The Universal Carrier was
weapons. Shown below are th
the Vickers Mk I, and a view
(M.O.D. Library, author's collec

...kers Mk I was transported on
...e shown on these pages. At top
...lion of the Welsh Regiment
... on limbers, 1914. These were
...bered, G.S." seen at top right.
... of a M.G. company, Macedonia
...ck saddlery, shown on mules
...r 1923. With "mechanisation"
...edweight" trucks of various
...edfords, carrying the Royal
...n of 5 Corps — England 1940.

...d for the carriage of many
...orms of vehicle mounting for
... towage of equipment in 1944.
...d Welch Regiment Museum.)

COLOUR PLATE C

In June 1945 the 5th Parachute Brigade (7, 12 and 13 Para) were shipped from the United Kingdom to the Far East. They took with them the clothing and equipment specially developed for the Japanese war, including 1944 pattern equipment and "carriers, manpack, G.S.", both of which are being carried by the central figure — a Corporal "No. 1" of the 7th (Light Infantry) battalion, Parachute Regiment.

Manpack frames greatly assisted the assembly of loads for what was termed a "long carry". (A "short carry" meant unloading the Vickers and its equipment from the vehicle and carrying it to the gun position. This could be several yards or several miles. A "long carry" meant just that!) Strapped to our subject's frame are the Vickers M.M.G., spare parts case, a liner of ammunition and the Corporal's pack — a weight in excess of 80 pounds. Airborne and Commando units retained Vickers machine guns during World War Two, preferring their more immediate availability.

At the feet of the 7 Para N.C.O. are items mentioned in the text, a Barr and Stroud rangefinder, an aiming post and the box containing a night aiming lamp. The rangefinder was an optical instrument which measured the range to likely targets, reference points or map features. In various "marks" it served alongside the Vickers throughout its service life, as evidenced by the photographs at left. (Top, Ypres 1917. Note the Second-Lieutenant in the "Tommy" jacket taking compass bearings. Centre, before Monte Cassino, 1944, engaging a target at about 2,400 yards. Below, the M.M.G. platoon of 3 Para, Trucial Oman early 1960s. Note the director on its tripod between the two guns. (Author's collection and Joe Lyall.) The aiming post — and the lamp hung on it in darkness — provided a reference point from which angles of deflection and elevation could be measured by means of the dial sight, thus enabling a number of recorded fire tasks to be performed by day or night.

The figure at left depicts a Sergeant instructor in machine gunnery of the 6th Cheshires, 44th Division, 1942. Note the "regimental" field service cap of the Cheshires, titles, "battle insignia" and "M.G." badge worn to indicate instructor status.

At right is depicted a Vickers "No. 1" of the 1st Royal Northumberland Fusiliers, Egypt 1940. Note the helmet "V" of the old "Fifth Fusiliers", the sand-coloured paint on helmet and barrel casing, the pistol equipment of a "No. 1" and the spare parts case.

Insignia shown in detail features, (left to right) the cap badge of the Manchesters, the battle insignia of the 7th R.N.F. — 59th Division, the cap badge of the Kensingtons and the battle insignia of the 1st Middlesex, 15th (Scottish) Division.

Plate C

COLOUR PLATE D

The main figure on this plate depicts a private soldier Vickers M.M.G. "No. 2" of the 1st Battalion Cameron Highlanders — Aden 1957. Our subject is carrying the gun to where the "No. 1" is setting up the tripod in order to bring the Vickers into action. Following him from the transport (in this case Landrovers and trailers) the other gun numbers will bring up ammunition and the condenser can. Note the regimental insignia, and '44 pattern equipment pistol set.

The second figure depicts the Vickers M.M.G. platoon commander of the 1st Battalion Royal Hampshires, 7th Armoured Division, British Army of the Rhine, 1953. At this time extensive field firing was carried out in B.A.O.R. involving weapons and troops of all arms in realistic battle situations. Young soldiers were thus able to experience the sight, the sound and the fairly close proximity of artillery, mortar and machine gun support. Our subject is depicted "laying out" such a shoot, in which stringent peacetime safety rules were observed. Range tables, compass and map are evident and these formed the basis for the considerable calculations that went into the planning and preparation of M.M.G. fire tasks. Note the regimental distinctions, '37 pattern equipment and Armoured Corps map board.

Detail shown at the bottom of the plate includes the skill-at-arms badge for the best machine gunner of the junior ranks of a unit (late 1920s and 1930s), the badge of the S.A.S.C., or Small Arms School Corps, who provided instructional staff for the Vickers machine gun training establishments during the weapon's service, and a comparison between the early (rivetted) pattern of belt and the later (woven) type.

The photograph at top, right shows a Vickers of the 1st Manchesters in Malaya, 1941. Note the first-pattern flash eliminator fitted over the muzzle attachment. (Author's collection.)

At bottom, right is a Vickers M.M.G. of the 1st Welch in a bunker position, Korea 1952. By this time the Korean War had become a static, positional conflict, said by observers to be reminiscent of the Great War. Note the dial sight and the woven type of ammunition belt. The gun is depressed to shoot into the valley of no-mans-land. (Welch Regiment Museum.)

At centre is a diagram of the Vickers dial sight. Fitted to a mounting on the left of the gun, the deflection and elevation (range) of a registered task were set on the sight. The lensatic sight was then "aimed" at the aiming post or lamp and bubbles were levelled by moving the traverse and elevation mechanism of the gun and tripod. In this way the Vickers could rapidly engage a succession of targets as ordered.

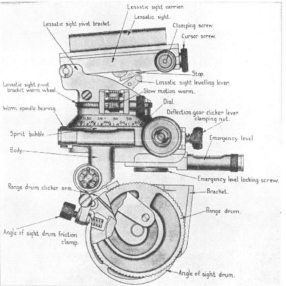

In the years between the world wars Vickers Mk I machine guns were decentralised, with each infantry battalion having a machine gun company. Above, men of 'D' (M.G.) Company, 1st Welch, clean their Vickers guns, Aldershot 1932. (Welch Regiment Museum.)

and skill. ("Preliminary" training for a gun number took nearly two months in 1939, when the manual listed eleven pages of Immediate Action and stoppages.) Repairs taught for the Vickers included fitting spare discs for the muzzle attachment, fitting auxilliary packing glands, adjustment of sights, repairing perforated barrel casings and repairing belts. The spare parts wallet for each gun contained 31 items including pliers, punches, screwdriver and mirror. The spare parts case included a spring balance, spare lock, clearing plug, spare fuzee spring and combination tool. The spare parts box contained 136 items including two spare feed blocks, fuzee with chain, belt repairing tool, hammer, screwdriver, spanners and sundry other "spares".

With skilled gun numbers to keep the Vickers firing, equally skilled fire controllers were needed to direct the fire onto the target according to the task.

These tasks might include direct fire at visible targets, fire over the heads of own troops, indirect fire at targets not visible from the gun position or fire at targets obscured by night, smoke or fog. To aid the fire controllers there were Barr and Stroud rangefinders, range tables, "maps of a scale not less than 1/50,000", compasses, protractors, clinometers, levels, directors and plotters. Fire control computations for indirect fire were layed on the Vickers by means of direction dials, elevating wheels, aiming posts, aiming lamps, night sights and dial sights. By 1940 an artilleryman would have instantly recognised, and been familiar with, all the plotting, sighting and laying apparatus available to a Vickers M.G. platoon.

From early in the Great War tactical thinking moved away from machine guns employed singly or in pairs, stress being placed on "battery" grouping. In

the great set-piece attacks of 1916 and 1917 hundreds of Vickers machine guns fired millions of rounds on barrage and harrassing tasks in the manner of the artillery. Even by 1942 the minimum fire unit for indirect fire was considered to be a platoon of 4 guns.

The four main defects of the Vickers machine gun in the Great War were not tackled until the late 1930s or early 1940s. New muzzle attachments were developed to eliminate flash, a dial sight was designed for the gun and new belts — filled and sealed in "liners" in the factory — were developed. The recommendation to adopt the "Spandau" sled-mounting was, however, not put into effect. Inferior ammunition — mostly foreign made — had been purchased in great quantity during the Great War and caused many stoppages when used in M.G.s. It became necessary to select ammunition for M.G. use, leaving the remainder for use in

(continued on page 24)

Smoke, steam and muzzle blast! All are evident in the photographs on this page. Right, a Vickers of an 8th Army machine gun battalion engages a target at about 2,000 yards — Italy, early 1945. Above, steam billows from a condenser can as a 1st Royal Northumberland Fusilier's Vickers engages a target at about a mile — Derna, North Africa, 1941. Below, a Vickers of the 1st Manchesters in action, Reichswald, Germany, 1945. (Author's collection and Welch Regiment Museum.)

Above, a Vickers Mk I of the 9th Royal Northumberland Fusiliers field firing, U.K., 1941. (Months later this unit — M.G. battalion to the 18th Division — passed into Japanese captivity on the capitulation of Singapore.) Note the dial sight, dial sight case beside the "number one's" leg, swivels on the water-jacket and first-pattern flash eliminator. Note also the red "V" of the "5th Fusiliers" on the steel helmets. Below, an illustration taken from a 1944 Vickers Mk I machine gun manual shows the gun mounted on a slope. Sights are set for about 1,000 yards. Note the "parabellum" flash eliminator, ammunition in "liners" and the regimental flash of the Cheshires on the Corporal's sleeve. (I.W.M. and M.O.D. Library.)

Above, the same gun and team as in the previous photograph demonstrate the positions adopted for firing down a slope. Note the spare parts case carried by the "number two". Below, a Vickers machine gun section of 1 Commando Brigade, Wesel, Germany, 1945. Commando and Airborne formations held Vickers machine guns within units, in the case of the Commandos in the "heavy weapons troop". (1 Commando Brigade had No. 3, No. 6, No. 45 (RM) and No. 46 (RM) Commandos under command.) (M.O.D. Library and I.W.M.)

Above, men of the 29th Infantry Brigade clean their Vickers, Korea, April 1951. By this time the Vickers M.M.G. had again been decentralised, and was issued on the scale of 6 guns per infantry battalion. Note the way in which the condenser tube has been stowed for carriage. A former Vickers M.M.G. section Sergeant of the 1st Glosters described to the author the physical and technical difficulties encountered by machine gunners in Korea, but recalled with satisfaction neutralising an enemy artillery O.P. at extreme range (4,500 yards). This was verified from the map and range-finding instruments, and elevation was set on the guns by means of a clinometer. At extreme ranges bullets would rise several hundred feet above the line of sight and descend steeply on the target in a cone.

Below are two instruments used in 1915 for indirect and distant gun-laying. At left is a device for measuring angle of sight, and at right an "Abney level", on which the pendulum and scale of a simple clinometer are clearly visible. Later Vickers clinometers were more robust and used levelling bubbles to measure up to 20 degrees of elevation or depression. (I.W.M. and Joe Garabant.)

A Vickers medium machine gun of the 1st Buffs engaging a target on a hillside at about a mile, Dhala, Aden 1958. Judging from the empty liners, much ammunition has been fired. The tripod beyond the gun supports the "Director, No. 4 Mk II", a fire controller's instrument. Shortage of water for the gun's cooling system could be a problem in arid countries. When this situation arose urine was usually used, making the gun position an unpopular place when the Vickers "boiled up" and started to steam! The gun's coolant would boil after about 600 rounds had been fired rapidly and would evaporate at the rate of $1\frac{1}{2}$ pints for each 1,000 rounds fired. Steam was passed via a tube into a condenser can — visible below the gun muzzle — cooled into liquid and poured back into the barrel casing. (Author's collection.)

rifles. In 1916 a Mk VII z round with a nitro-cellulose propellant was developed for the Vickers. The round was more reliable than the cordite Mk VII, but in 1938 a Mk VIII z nitro round was introduced for the gun, its boat-tailed ("streamlined") bullet increasing the maximum effective range of the Vickers to 4,500 yards.

Despite the "mechanisation for a mobile war" that had taken place prior to 1939, some M.G. units were required to transport their Vickers on pack transport during World War Two, notably in Burma and Italy. Two mules were required for each gun and 7 boxes (1,750 rounds) of ammunition, each animal carrying slightly more than 200 pounds. No mules were available to carry Vickers M.M.G.s and their ammo up Korean hillsides from 1950 to 1953, but locals serving as porters to the Commonwealth units did just as well.

It was in Korea that the Vickers once more came into its own in the desperate fighting up to the summer of 1951, and in the "trench warfare" that endured until the Armistice.

The Reconnaissance/Machine Gun platoon of the 1st Glosters fired their Vickers M.M.G.s for the last time in Libya in 1963. The battalion watched as the elderly weapons shot out their streams of ball ammunition interspersed with the odd round of tracer which burned out long before the bullets struck the desert surface at extreme range. It was a sad occasion, but no-one watching the demonstration could fail to recognise the power, the range and the sheer lethality of these "museum pieces".

"The author wishes to record his thanks to the following for their help in the production of this publication — Ministry of Defence Library, Prince Consort's Library, Mr Joe Garabrant and Mr Byron "Spud" Murphy."

Creative
DECORAT
PAINTING

A J.B. Fairfax Press Publication

EDITORIAL
Managing Editor: Judy Poulos
Editorial Assistant: Ella Martin
Editorial Coordinator: Margaret Kelly

PHOTOGRAPHY
Steve Tanner, Di Lewis, Andrew Elton

ILLUSTRATIONS
Margaret Metcalfe

DESIGN AND PRODUCTION
Manager: Sheridan Carter
Layout: Gavin Murrell
Finished Art: Steve Joseph

Published by J.B. Fairfax Press Pty Limited
80-82 McLachlan Avenue
Rushcutters Bay 2011 Australia
A.C.N. 003 738 430

Formatted by J.B. Fairfax Press Pty Limited
Printed by Toppan Printing Co,
Hong Kong

JBFP 154
CREATIVE DECORATIVE PAINTING
ISBN 1 86343 105 5

DISTRIBUTION AND SALES
Newsagents Direct Distributors
150 Bourke Road, Alexandria NSW 2015
Tel: (02) 353 9911 Fax: (02) 669 2305

Sales Enquiries:
J.B. Fairfax Press Pty Limited
Tel: (02) 361 6366 Fax: (02) 360 6262

Contents

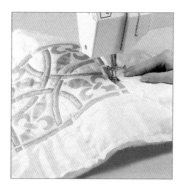

42 Furniture Facelifts

Toy Chest

Sponged Cabinet

Marbled Plant Stand

Stencilled Bedroom

Bed Drapes

Cane Chair

Chest of Drawers

Wall Border

Ribbon Bows

Florentine Hallway

Stencilled Bathroom

Transform your home with these decorative painting and stencilling projects for every room.

DECORATIVE PAINTING

Somewhere deep inside all of us is an artist just waiting for the opportunity to shine. In the past this has remained an unrealised ambition for most people. These days, thanks to the arrival of easy-to-use, almost foolproof, paints and the revival of traditional decorative techniques, anyone can be an artist.

Just as exciting is the discovery that you can use an enormous variety of objects and surfaces for your canvas. You can transform just about anything with some paint and a little imagination. Craft shops sell an increasing variety of objects specifically for this purpose, such as lidded balsa wood boxes, plain china, craft paper lampshades, picture frames and wooden items of various kinds. If you are unsure of where to find these items, check the advertisements in your favourite craft magazine. Remember, too, that decorative painting techniques will do wonders for that much-used treasure stored in the garage.

In this book, you will find a host of easy-to-do projects that cover painting on glass, fabric, plaster, wood and ceramics. The full-sized templates for the designs are on the pattern sheet, ready for you to trace off. You don't need to have any special skills – if you can trace a design and hold a paintbrush, you can achieve anything in this book.

CHOOSING YOUR DESIGN

If you are a novice, you will probably feel more comfortable using a template exactly as it is given. As you gain confidence and skill, experiment with the designs, changing elements or colours until you find an arrangement that pleases you. Sources of inspiration are all around you. As well as books, look out for tile and fabric patterns, china designs, gift-wrapping paper, ceramic tiles and wallpaper patterns.

Once you have chosen your design, you may find that it is not the size you need. The simplest way to enlarge or reduce a design is with a photocopier. If this is not possible, you will need to use the grid method which is described on page 7.

TRANSFERRING THE DESIGN

Some designs can be transferred quite easily to the object you are painting – particularly so when an irregular, freehand look is called for or if the design is very simple.

If you have a more complex design where some exactness is required, there is a method to help you. First, trace the design from the pattern sheet on to a piece of tracing paper. Next, place the tracing over the area it is to occupy and tape it in place with masking tape. Slip a piece of graphite paper (such as Transitrace) between the tracing and the surface and go over the lines with a sharp pencil or stylus. This will transfer the outline to the surface with lines of graphite which you can erase when the painting is complete. These graphite papers come in a light and a dark form so you can choose one that is appropriate to the surface you are painting on.

MATERIALS

These days there is an enormous variety of paint and paint-type products on the market. For best results, you should always choose a product that is specifically formulated for the surface you are working on. Some products are multi-purpose and are therefore particularly useful to have in your collection.

Always try to buy the best brushes you can afford and look after them. Clean your brushes after every use – in mineral turpentine (for solvent-based paints) or water (for water-based paints). For more tips on looking after your brushes, see page 9.

You will need a variety of paintbrush sizes, from narrow liner brushes to quite large flat brushes, depending on the projects you choose. Begin with the brushes you need for your first project, then add to your collection as you go.

CHOOSING PAINTS
Acrylic Paints
The easiest paints to use, acrylic paints, are available in a huge range of colours and sizes of containers (from tubes to large cans). Because they are water-based, clean-up is simple. Take care to attend to

this quickly, because once the paint has dried, it will be as permanent as any solvent-based paint and will certainly ruin your brushes.

Acrylic paints can be applied to almost any surface and do not need primer or undercoat. They are equally suitable for indoor or outdoor use and are fully water-proof when dry.

Ceramic Paints

Ceramic paints should be used for items which are largely decorative. Available in a wide range of colours, they give a shiny finish to ceramics, glass, metal and even wood.

They can be coated with a ceramic varnish to give an even glossier and somewhat more durable surface. Do not put items painted with these paints in the dishwasher; wash them carefully by hand in warm soapy water.

Fabric Paints

There are a number of types of fabric paints available today and most are easy to apply. Read the manufacturer's information on the tube, pot or pen to find the one that is suitable for your purpose. Most fabric paints work best when applied to a white or cream surface but some will colour a darker surface quite well. The range of colours is excellent and includes metallic shades as well.

Fabric pens are a very easy option if you want a little more control of the colour, such as outlining or writing. Take care to tape your fabric down when using pens or straight-from-the-tube paints as the fabric can become wrinkled, making it difficult for you to work.

When considering fabric painting, check out the 'puff' type paints and dimensional paints as well; they can give unusual highlights to your work.

Painting on silk requires a slightly different

Above: Tiles, wrapping paper, fabric, books and china can all provide a rich source of painting designs

technique. It is crucial to use a frame when painting silk, in order to hold the silk firm and to keep it off the work surface. Special frames are available for this purpose or you can make your own, and special silk pins are used for fastening the silk to the frame. Once the silk is stretched quite tightly in the frame, tape the tracing of your design under the silk and trace over all the outlines with gutta, a gum-like substance. The gutta acts as a barrier, preventing the paint from spreading to an area where it is not wanted. The silk paints (or dyes) flow on to the silk and will flow through any breaks in the gutta. Make sure the gutta lines are continuous and any outlines are closed. Leave the gutta to dry for at least an hour before you begin applying the paint.

Once the paints are dry, the fabrics should be heat-set to make the paint permanent. There are a number of ways you can do this, including steaming, pressing with a warm iron, using your hairdryer, chemical solutions and even microwaving. Follow the manufacturer's instructions and choose the right method for the paints you have used.

Glass Paints

Ideal for decorative items, glass paints give the lovely effect of stained glass. Either solvent- or water-based, they should be applied carefully with a soft clean brush and left to dry for at least a day in a dust-free place. Because the paints do not flow as easily as some others do, a little practice is required to master their use. To achieve a strong deep colour, you may need to apply two coats

Before you begin painting the glass, wash it in warm soapy water, rinse, then dry it thoroughly. To remove any dust or adhering particles, wipe the glass with methylated spirits.

You can use glass paints to decorate china and ceramics but they are not suitable for items which need to cope with a lot of wear and tear. Do not put painted glass in the dishwasher; wash it by hand in lukewarm soapy water.

Other Paints

In addition to these general groups of paint products, there are other products that are quite suitable, such as felt pens. These are very inexpensive and easy to use on a variety of surfaces, such as paper, wood and plaster.

Stencilling paints or crayons are formulated specially to use with stencil brushes in the dabbing or pouncing motion that is required for stencilling. (See page 9 for more on stencilling paints.)

Varnish

Once you have completed your painting, you will need to decide whether to add a coat of varnish and, if you do, whether it should be matt or glossy. The choices are up to you but, generally, a coat of varnish is helpful in giving an extra layer of protection. Make sure your paints are completely dry before you varnish and that the product you use is compatible with the paints and surface it is covering.

Left: Tracing a design off a piece of fabric
Above: Drawing a stencil design from a tracing, leaving 'bridges' in place

STENCILLING

Welcome to the world of stencilling – one of the simplest and most satisfying ways of decorating with paint. Anyone can be a skilful stencil artist, even without the usual talents we associate with the term 'artist'. This book is like a stencil supermarket for the enthusiast. We provide you with a number of wonderful stencil designs – all you have to do is trace them and then cut out your stencil, following the detailed instructions for making stencils on the following pages.

Stencilling is a means of transferring a design, usually a regularly repeating design, to a surface, by applying paint through holes that have been cut out for that purpose. In fact, anything with holes in it, like a piece of lace or a doily, can function as a stencil.

The paints that are used are naturally dictated by the surface to be stencilled. The surface can be made of just about anything – plaster, fabric, wood, china, paper and more.

While stencilling is a very traditional means of decorating, the technique works just as well in a modern setting where it can add considerable warmth and character to an otherwise fairly sterile room*.

The process is not difficult to master. First decide on the motif for your stencil design. Look around and you will find you are surrounded by potential stencil designs – on your favourite china cup, the material of a dress, a book, or a wallpaper pattern. You could even design your own pattern for a stencil. Many people simplify matters even further by painting a ready-to-use stencil. These are becoming more and more popular and are available at quite reasonable cost from craft shops.

Using a popular stencil does not mean that your work will look the same as that of someone else who has used the same stencil. Each person adds their own unique mark, in the colours they choose, the way in which they apply the paint and where they place the stencil.

You can stencil just about anything, but if you are a beginner, choose something small for your first project. Finishing that, and basking in the admiration of family and friends, will encourage you to continue, and to become more adventurous with each project.

See a stencilled room on page 50

HOW TO STENCIL

Tracing the design

First choose your stencil design. This can be a motif from a book, a piece of fabric or wallpaper, gift wrapping paper, or your own imagination.

If the design needs to be reduced or enlarged, the simplest method is to use a photocopier. If you do not have access to a photocopier, you will have to use the grid method. To do this, draw up a squared grid over the design. Draw another grid with the same number of squares on a fresh sheet of paper. If you want to enlarge the design, make these squares larger than those in the first grid. For example, if you want to double the size of the design, make the squares on the second grid twice the size of the first one. If you want to reduce the size, make the second grid smaller. Now, draw into each square of the second grid, the contents of that square on the first grid, matching the points where outlines cross the grid lines. Don't try to draw in the details until all the main outlines are drawn. Continue in this way until you have transferred the entire design to the new grid.

Making the stencil

If the design is to be used just as it is, with no changes to size or elements of the design, and if you are using clear acetate for your stencil, then it can be traced straight on to the acetate. To make a stencil, trace in the outlines of the elements adding small 'bridges' so that colour areas are enclosed by a continuous line.

For a multi-coloured design, you will find it easier to work if you make a separate stencil for each colour. Trace the entire design on to each stencil, using solid lines for all the parts in one colour and dotted lines for the other outlines. These dotted lines will serve as registration marks for matching up the stencils. For a repeating design, such as a wall pattern or border, add some registration marks, or the dotted outline of the next element at the edges of the design, as well.

Cut out the areas of the design that are to be painted, with a scalpel or sharp craft knife. A self-healing rubber mat will hold the stencil material in place while you work. To ensure accurate cutting, use only the tip of the knife, moving it towards you. Begin

7

cutting in the centre of a space and work towards the edges, turning the acetate rather than the scalpel to cut around curves.

Painting the stencil

Mark with a pencil any guidelines on the surface to be stencilled, such as the true vertical or the distance from a given edge. If the stencil is a repeating design, such as a border, mark in the position of each repeat of the design so that you can make any adjustments to the spacing.

To ensure a clean outline, the stencil must sit flush with the surface to be painted and be held there firmly. Tape the first stencil at its first position with low-tack masking tape.

Choose a paint that is appropriate to the surface to be stencilled. Pour a little of the paint on to an old plate or saucer – stencilling works best when the paint is used quite sparingly. Dip only the ends of the bristles of the stencil brush in the paint, then wipe off any excess paint on to a piece of kitchen paper.

Apply small amounts of paint with a dabbing or pouncing motion. Make sure that you use enough paint to make a clear outline at the edges, but vary the depth of paint across the stencil to give an interestingly shaded effect. Don't use the paint too thickly.

The best fabric for stencilling is a close-woven natural one, such as cotton or silk. Wash and iron the fabric before pinning it out on a work surface that has been protected with sheets of absorbent paper.

When you have large areas to cover and are looking for a soft mottled effect, stencil with a sponge. Always dampen the sponge first before picking up a little paint from the palette. Remove any excess paint on to kitchen paper before you apply the paint with a light dabbing motion.

Clean your equipment with either water or a solvent, depending on the type of paint you have used. It is also very important to clean your stencil often as you work – paint build-up can distort the outlines and even block small holes.

MATERIALS

Tracing Paper and Pencil

Ideally, you will be able to trace your stencil design on to the actual stencil material, but there will be occasions when an intermediate step is required and it is then that you will need tracing paper and pencil. If you are going to adjust the design or isolate a part of it, you should trace it first on to tracing paper, then make whatever changes you wish before making your stencil.

To enlarge a motif, first trace it onto a grid

The Stencil

For a long time, stencils have been made using thick manilla card coated with a 1:1 mixture of mineral turpentine and boiled linseed oil. The treated sheets of card are hung to dry and the excess coating carefully wiped off before use. The sheets are inexpensive and easy to work with, but they have the disadvantage of being opaque so you can't match up design elements or 'see where you are going'.

These days, clear plastic or acetate on rolls or sheets is often used for making stencils instead of manilla card. Choose an acetate that is thick enough to stand up to the wear and tear but not so thick that it is difficult to cut. Because these materials are transparent, they eliminate the need for tracing the design on to tracing paper and then transferring it to the stencil material. You can trace the design directly on to the acetate with a fineline permanent marker pen.

Sharp Craft Knife

Once the design is traced on to the acetate, you will need to cut out those areas that will be covered by paint. Scissors are not suitable; you will need a sharp craft knife or scalpel (available from craft shops).

Cutting Mat

A self-healing rubber mat for cutting on is quite useful but not essential. If you will be using one frequently, it is probably quite a good investment, as the rubber surface not only protects your work surface but your blades as well. The mats are printed with grid lines which are useful for drawing and cutting straight lines.

Masking Tape

A roll of masking tape in two or three widths is a must for stencilling. You will need tape for holding tracings in place, for securing stencils, and for masking surfaces that you wish to protect from paint. The tape is also very useful for running repairs to torn or damaged stencils – much easier than making a new one.

It is possible to buy low-tack masking tape which can be removed without damaging the painted surface. Whether you use low-tack masking tape or the ordinary variety, always exercise great care when pulling the tape away from the surface.

Stencil Brushes

Stencilling requires special brushes that are quite different from ordinary paintbrushes in that the bristle end is flat rather than pointed. This shape is dictated by the way in which stencils are painted – with a dabbing or 'pouncing' motion rather than by stroking.

Always choose the best brushes you can afford and look after them well. Clean them after every use (either in water or solvent – depending on the paint used). If you clean them in solvent, wash them afterwards in a mild detergent solution and dry the bristles with kitchen paper. Never leave paint on the brushes and never store them soaking in water or solvent. Once they are clean and dry, store them standing, with bristles up, in a jar or similar container.

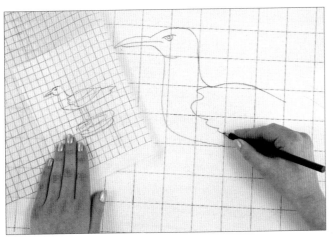

Enlarging the motif by copying it on to a larger grid

Sponges

Natural sponges are very useful for stencilling where the design is quite open and where a soft-textured appearance is desired. Clean your sponges in the same way as the brushes and, when dry, store them in a suitable container.

Paints

You can use just about any paint for stencilling; your choice will usually depend on the surface. There are paints available which are specially made for stencilling. They have the advantage of being fast-drying, allowing you to paint, remove the stencil and replace it in its next position more quickly than you can with most other paints. Stencil paints come in a wide range of colours and can also be mixed to create any colour you wish.

For stencilling on fabric, you can choose from a wide range of paint. Some have the consistency of a thick liquid, others are in powder form, and others are applied directly from a bottle. To allow the item to be washed, the paint needs to be made permanent by fixing with heat. Follow the manufacturer's instructions to heat-set the particular paint you have used.

Special ceramic paints are available for use on tiles, china, ornaments and glass. While these paints are technically permanent, you will need to treat the stencilled object with a little care.

Many other paints can be used for stencilling, including ordinary house paints (either water or oil-based). Cans of spray paint, made for motor vehicles, are very simple to use where a quick overall effect is required on walls, metal surfaces or plastics. If you do choose spray paints, take extra care to mask off the surrounding area with drop-cloths or newspaper before you begin; the spray can travel a surprising distance.

Artists acrylic colours make great stencil paints, particularly for surfaces which need to be flexible.

Ruler

A long plastic ruler is very useful to mark straight lines for placement of the design or for drawing in registration marks for matching up stencils.

Fabric Painting

Painting on fabric is not a modern fad – it has been known since ancient times. These days, with the variety of paints and fabrics available, the possibilities for fabric painting are limitless. Painting your own fabric is a wonderful way of stamping your individuality on your environment.

The most common way to use fabric painting is to decorate a piece of fabric, which is then made up in the usual way into a garment or item of soft furnishing. The other method is to take an existing garment or piece of soft furnishing and then paint a design or motif on it.

Choose paints that are suitable to the project you have in mind, taking into account such factors as wearability and washability. Most fabric paints must be set or 'fixed' with heat to make them permanent and washable.

The delightful tea cloth opposite has been stencilled in a design that mirrors the china pattern. To make a cloth like this, isolate an element or two of your favourite china pattern. It need not be an exact copy but should be harmonious and the colours should match as closely as possible. In this case, separate stencils were made for the border pattern and the corner motif. These were then stencilled around the cloth and napkins as shown. When the paint was dry, the cloth and napkins were pressed on the wrong side with a hot iron to fix the paints, following the manufacturer's instructions.

When you are planning your cloth, take note of which parts of the cloth will be visible when it is laid on the table. Don't waste your efforts on those parts which will not be seen.

PAINTED SILK SCARF

Silk painting, which is much easier than it looks, is not only a very satisfying hobby but also a wonderful source of presents for friends and family.

Left: Tracing the design
Above: The completed scarf

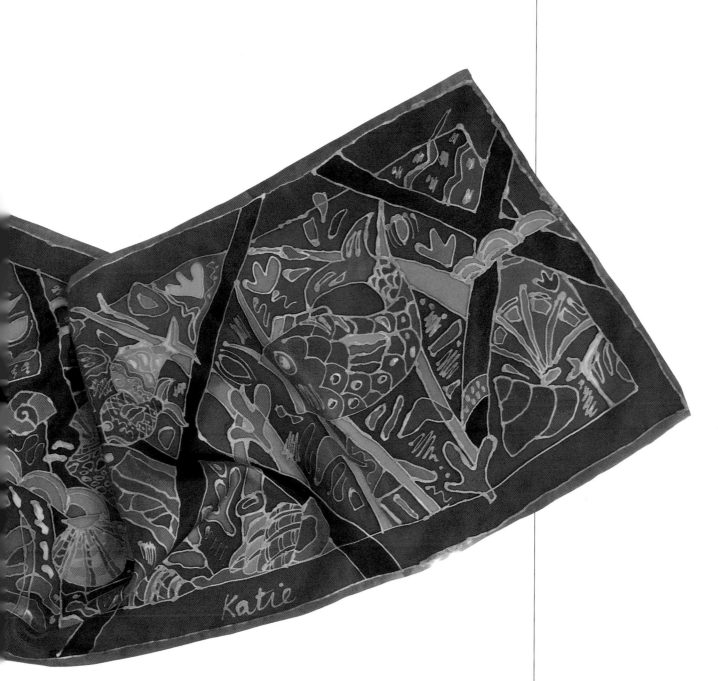

MATERIALS
tracing paper and pencil
90 cm square or 30 cm x 120 cm of
*   plain silk (Habutai no. 8)*
silk frame
silk pins
masking tape
clear gutta
silk paints
soft paintbrush

INSTRUCTIONS
See the design on the Pull Out
Pattern Sheet.

1 Enlarge the design from the
  Pattern Sheet to the required size to
cover your piece of silk. If you do not
have access to a photocopier to enlarge
the design, use the grid method (see
page 7).

2 Stretch the length of silk over the
  frame, using special silk pins.
Frames suitable for this purpose are
available from craft shops, ready for you
to assemble. A frame is essential for silk
painting as it keeps the silk quite taut
and raised off the work surface.

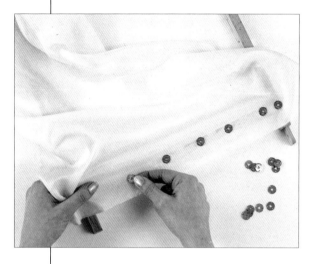

3 Tape the design to the frame underneath the silk so that you can see it clearly through the fabric. Trace in the main outlines with the pencil.

4 Follow the pencil lines with the gutta (a gum-like material which serves to separate areas of colour, preventing one colour from bleeding into another). For the gutta to be effective the lines must be continuous; any gaps will allow the silk paint to seep through. Allow the gutta to dry for an hour before beginning to paint.

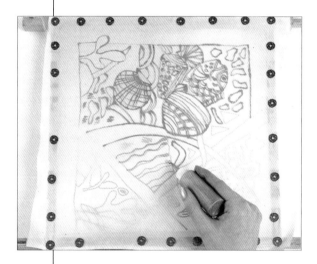

5 Apply the paints with a soft brush, applying the colour between the lines of gutta and letting the paint creep up to the lines. Clean the brush in water before dipping it in the next colour.

6 When the painting is complete and the paint is dry, you can fix the colours by one of the following methods: iron on the back of the silk, steam the silk in a pressure cooker or professional steamer, or use a combination of microwave and fixative. Be guided by the instructions on the paint bottles. Your scarf is now ready to hem.

Top left: Pinning the silk to the frame
Centre left: Outlining the design with the gutta
Left: Painting the design

*Quilted silk cushions
(see page 16)*

15

QUILTED SILK CUSHIONS

*These elegant
cream silk
cushions have
been stencilled
with metallic
fabric paints and
then quilted for a
really luxurious
effect.*

MATERIALS

*48 cm square of cream silk for the
    cushion front
2 pieces of cream silk, each
    25 cm x 48 cm, for the cushion
    back
brown wrapping paper
masking tape
sheets of clear acetate for the stencils
sharp craft knife
cutting board (optional)
fineline permanent marker pen
stencil brush
metallic fabric paints
old saucer or plate for a palette
48 cm square of polyester wadding
cream sewing thread
25 cm zipper
30 cm cushion insert*

INSTRUCTIONS

See the design on the Pull Out Pattern
Sheet.
1.5 cm seams allowed.

1 Fold the silk square into halves
and then into quarters. Press in
the creases.

2 Trace the stencil design from the
Pattern Sheet on to the acetate
with the fineline pen, marking in the
horizontal and vertical lines on the
design. These indicate the centre of
the complete design.

3 Cut out the areas to be painted
with the craft knife.

4 Tape the silk square on to the
work surface (which has been
protected with layers of the brown
wrapping paper). Position the stencil
on the silk square, matching the
pressed lines with the drawn lines on
the stencil. Tape the stencil in place
on the silk square.

5 Place a small amount of the
metallic fabric paint on the saucer
or plate. Load the stencil brush with a
small amount of paint and, with a
dabbing motion, begin to colour in the
stencil. Allow the paint to dry before
lifting the stencil.

6 Reposition the stencil around the
silk square, each time lining up
the lines with the creases and allowing
the paint to dry before moving on to
the next position. When all the painting is complete, leave to dry for
twenty-four hours, then set the paint
with a medium-to-hot iron.

7 Baste the square of polyester
wadding to the wrong side of the
painted silk square. Use several rows
of basting to ensure the layers are held
together securely.

8 Machine-quilt around some of the motifs or around all of them if you prefer.

9 Place the cushion backs with right sides together. Join them along one side with an 11.5 cm long seam at each end, leaving an opening in the middle for the zipper. Press the seam open. Sew the zipper into the opening and leave it open.

10 Place the cushion back and front together with right sides facing. Sew around the outside in a 1.5 cm seam. Trim the seams and turn the cushion to the right side through the zipper opening. Press lightly.

11 Stitch parallel rows around the cushion cover, stitching through all layers to make a 6 cm border all around.

12 Place the cushion insert inside the stencilled cover.

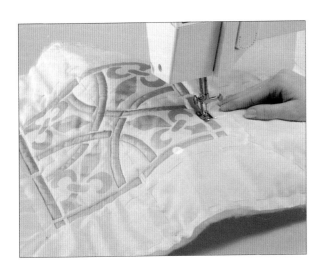

Far left: Lining up the stencil on the silk square
Above: Painting in the stencil design
Left: Quilting around the stencilled motifs

STENCILLED CURTAIN & TIE-BACK

A simple calico curtain takes on a new elegance with a padded and stencilled border and matching tie-back. The instructions given here are for making the border only. You will need to make up your own curtain when the border is attached.

Below: Painting in the stencil curtain design
Below right: Pinning the stencilled fabric over the interfacing
Far right: The completed curtain and tie-back

MATERIALS

sufficient calico
masking tape
firm interfacing (not iron-on)
tracing paper
pencil
sheets of clear acetate for the stencils
fineline permanent marker pen
sharp craft knife
newspaper
brown wrapping paper
fabric paint
old saucer or plate for a palette
stencil brush
piping (either readymade or make your own)
pelmet stiffening or very firm iron-on interfacing
pins
matching sewing thread
2 small brass rings

INSTRUCTIONS

See the design on the Pull Out Pattern Sheet.
1.5 cm seams allowed.

CURTAIN BORDER

1 Cut a piece of calico 25 cm wide and the length of the curtain. You will probably need to cut this down the length of the fabric so as to avoid any joins.

2 Trace the stencil design from the Pattern Sheet on to the acetate using the fineline pen. Cut out the stencil with the sharp knife.

3 Cover your work surface with newspaper with a sheet of brown wrapping paper on top. Tape the fabric strip to this work surface.

4 Position the stencil on one end of the strip, 4.5 cm from one long edge. Tape the stencil in place.

5 Pour a little of the fabric paint into the saucer. Load the stencil brush with a small amount of the paint and paint in the stencil design with a dabbing motion. Leave this section to dry before lifting the stencil and placing it on the next section to be

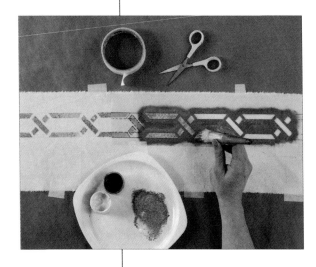
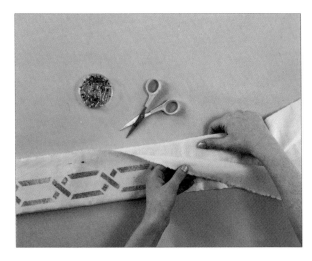

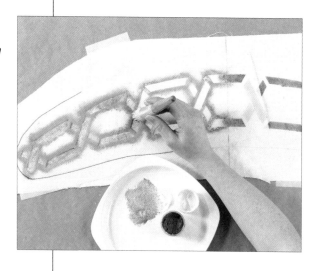

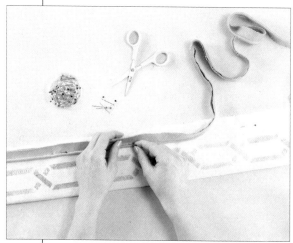

side of the curtain. Turn under the raw edge and slipstitch in place. Press well.

TIE-BACK

See the design on the Pull Out Pattern Sheet.

1 Cut two pieces of calico to the shape of the tie-back. Make the stencil in the same way as for the curtain border. Mark the outline of the tie-back and the halfway point.

2 Place the fabric and paint the stencil in the same way as for the curtain border, lifting the stencil (when the paint is dry) to paint in the second half, matching the pattern and the halfway points.

3 Cut the pelmet stiffening to the same shape as the tie-back. Remove the backing and press it on to the back of the stencilled calico. If using the iron-on interfacing, ignore the reference to the backing.

4 Trim away the excess calico, leaving a border 2 cm all around. Pin the piping to the calico with right sides facing and raw edges even. Clip the curves for ease. Stitch around the edge, close to the piping cord.

5 Remove the other backing and fold the seam allowance to the back. Clip the curves around the edge of the second piece of calico. Press the seam allowance to the wrong side. Place this piece on the back of the stencilled piece, with wrong sides together, and slipstitch into place. Press well. Sew a small brass ring to each end.

painted. When you reposition the stencil, take care to match the pattern exactly. Fix all the paint when it is dry.

6 Fold the fabric strip over double lengthways, with wrong sides together, placing a double thickness of interfacing in between. Pin the top layer of the calico and the interfacing together along the top edge.

7 Pin and stitch the piping to the top edge of the calico and the interfacing, with right sides together.

8 Pin the piped edge to the edge of your curtain, with right sides facing and raw edges even. Stitch close to the piping. Press the border out, folding the free edge to the wrong

Lacy bed linen (see page 22)

LACY BED LINEN

This is a delightful way to create the effect of exclusive lace-trimmed bed linen without the cost. All you need is a short length of lace which you can use to stencil the design on to pillowcases, sheets and quilt covers.

MATERIALS

plain sheet, pillowcase and quilt cover
length of lace, approximately 6 cm wide
narrow masking tape
newspaper
sheets of brown wrapping paper
pins
black fabric paint
water
mouth-spray diffuser
grey and peach satin ribbon, 1 cm and 1.5 cm wide
matching sewing thread

INSTRUCTIONS

1 Starting at one end of the wide hem at the top end of the sheet, pin the lace in place so that the decorative edge of the lace runs along the hemmed edge. Place a line of masking tape to cover the two short ends and the long straight edge of the lace.

2 Lay sheets of newspaper on your work surface to protect it from overspray. Lay brown paper on top of the newspaper to protect the bed linen from the dye in the newsprint.

3 Remove the pins from the lace and lay the section of sheet with the lace attached on to the brown paper. Cover all parts of the sheet, except for the lace section, with more brown paper, taping it in place.

4 In a small bottle, mix the black fabric paint with sufficient water to give a thin, very liquid consistency. Test the effect on a piece of scrap fabric, using the mouth-spray diffuser. Aim for a light-grey spotty texture that will spread through the holes in the lace on to the fabric. When you are confident with the colour and the diffuser, spray the lace-covered sheet in the same way. Leave to dry.

5 Move the length of lace along the sheet top, re-masking in the same way each time, until the whole length of the border is complete. Remove all the masking and leave the paint to dry for twenty-four hours.

6 Fix the paint using an iron set to the hottest setting appropriate for the sheet fabric.

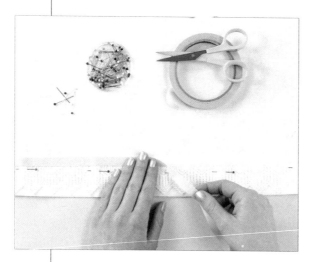

Top: Pinning and taping the lace in place
Right: Spraying the paint over the lace

7 Pin and stitch a length of 1 cm wide peach ribbon and 1.5 cm grey ribbon parallel to the edge of the lace, turning in the raw edges at the ends.

8 To decorate the pillowcases and quilt cover, mask, pin and spray the lace in the same way up to the first corner. At the corner, stick masking tape across the lace at an angle of 45° to mitre the corner. To continue along the next side, match up the pattern in the lace, mitring again at the corner with masking tape. Continue in this way until the border on all four sides is complete. Sew on peach satin ribbon as for the sheet.

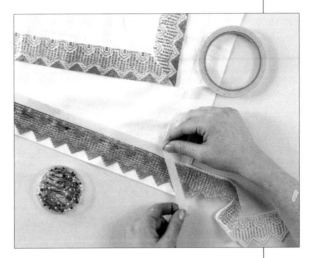

Top: Pinning the lengths of ribbon in place
Above: Mitre the corners on the pillowcases using masking tape

SPONGED CURTAINS

These simple floor-length curtains will add style to any modern living room and can be painted in any colour to complement your decor. The technique is so simple that even the children can paint a set of curtains for their own rooms.

MATERIALS

sufficient plain fabric
sheets of newspaper
masking tape
opaque black and white fabric paints
old saucer or plate for a palette
natural sponge

INSTRUCTIONS

1 Mask all around your work area with plenty of newspaper before you begin.

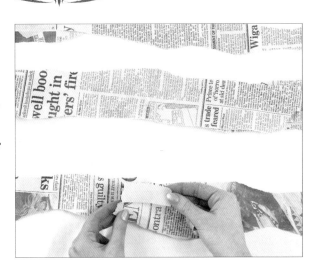

2 Tear sheets of newspaper into long irregularly shaped strips. Do not try to be too neat – the effect will be more dramatic if you allow a fair degree of variation.

3 Measure the area to be covered by the curtain. Your fabric will need to be twice the width of the window times the length to the floor, plus an allowance for hems and headings. Sew together enough fabric for your curtain but do not hem it or make the heading. Lay the fabric on the newspaper on the work area.

4 With masking tape, join together enough strips of newspaper to fit across the width of the fabric.

5 Leaving irregular gaps between the rows, stick the newspaper strips across the fabric, using little loops of masking tape to join the underside of the newspaper to the fabric. Cover the length of the fabric in this way, breaking up the rows with small 'islands' of paper as you move towards the top.

6 Pour some black paint on to the saucer or plate. Dip the damp sponge into the paint and, starting at the bottom, apply the paint between the rows of newspaper.

7 At the beginning of each new row, add a little white paint to the black, adding more white paint with each successive row so that the colour gradually lightens to grey as you work up the fabric. When you reach the top where you have the islands of paper, the colour should be quite light.

8 Allow the paint to dry before removing the strips of news-paper. Make the other curtain in the same way.

9 When the paint is dry, iron each piece of fabric on the wrong side to fix the colour. Finish making the curtains in the usual way.

Top left: Sticking irregularly shaped strips of newspaper aross the fabric
Centre left: Applying the paint with a sponge to the area between the paper strips
Bottom left: When the paint is dry, remove the strips of newspaper
Right: The completed curtains

Ornamental Painting

Painting your own designs on to kitchenware, glassware and ornaments will give your home a style that is quite unique. You will be able to turn inexpensive crockery from the supermarket into pieces you will be proud to display.

There are special paints available for decorating glass, ceramics, china and wood. Choose the right paint for the job and carefully follow the manufacturer's instructions. While the special ceramic and glass paints are relatively easy to use and are purpose-designed, they are not intended for items that will take a great deal of wear. Keep them for the more ornamental pieces.

More hardy are these painted terracotta pots which are definitely meant to be used. Paint the pots with simple designs of your own or isolate an element from any of the stencil designs given in this book. Stencilling a pot is quite simple as long as you take care to keep the stencil in contact with the pot and tape it in place while you work. You can make a very simple but effective design by masking off areas of the pot with masking tape and then sponging the exposed areas. Experiment with combinations of colours and designs to build up a collection of personalised pots like this to dress up a sunny corner. An oil-based mix of satin and gloss paints, or artists acrylic colours are both quite suitable for use on terracotta.

MEDITERRANEAN PLATTER

Bring all the sunshine of the Mediterranean into your home with this brightly coloured platter. This method of decorating is called 'resist painting' where a material (in this case the chinagraph pencil) prevents the paint from covering a certain area. To create this primitive design, you will need a mixture of glass and ceramic paints.

MATERIALS
plain white platter
glass paint, emerald green
ceramic paints in 4 colours of
    your choice
paintbrushes for applying the design
    and a larger one for the varnish
chinagraph pencil
soft dry cloth
mineral turpentine
ceramic varnish

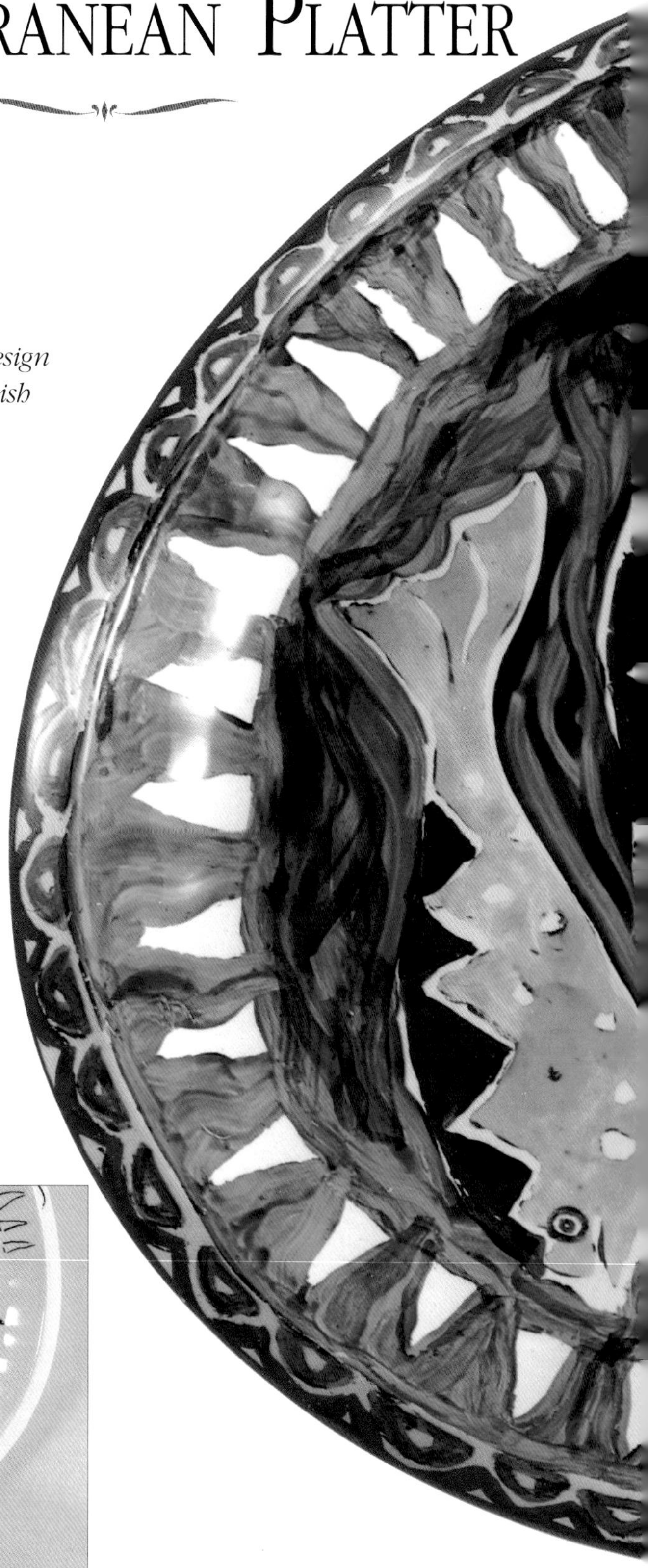

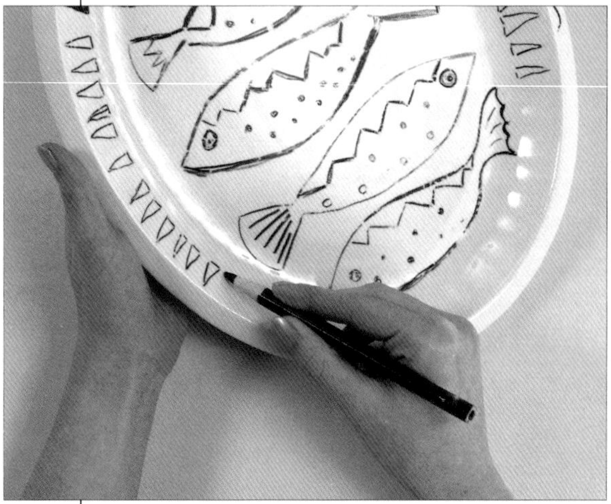

Right: Drawing the design with a chinagraph pencil

Above: The completed platter
Right: Painting the design with ceramic paints

29

INSTRUCTIONS

1 Practise drawing the fish motif on a scrap of paper until you are happy with it, then, using the chinagraph pencil, draw the design on to the platter. Those areas that are covered with the chinagraph will remain white on the finished platter.

2 Carefully paint in the fish with the ceramic paints. Keep the colours bright with a strong contrast such as deep blue and yellow, purple and orange, or black and gold.

3 Paint the border pattern in another pair of bright colours such as red and blue. Don't try to be too neat. This primitive style lends itself quite well to a little irregularity.

4 Paint the water around the fish in emerald green glass paint, applying the paint in a wave pattern to indicate water and waves. Use glass paint for this part of the design as it is more translucent than ceramic paint.

5 When the paint is completely dry, rub off the chinagraph lines with the soft dry cloth to reveal the white china beneath.

6 If you need to tidy up the edges of the platter, use the soft cloth soaked in mineral turpentine.

7 To protect your platter, paint it with a coat of ceramic varnish.

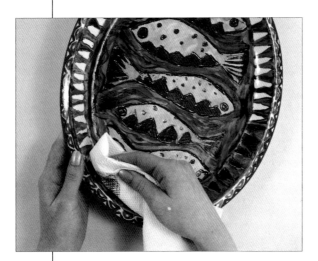

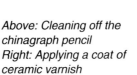

Above: Cleaning off the chinagraph pencil
Right: Applying a coat of ceramic varnish

SOPHISTICATED GLASSES

MATERIALS
scrap paper
pencil
wine glasses
*glass paint in the colours of
    your choice*
fine paintbrush

INSTRUCTIONS

1 Before you begin painting, it is a good idea to plan your design on some scrap paper. Don't be too restricted by this plan, just use it to decide what works well and what doesn't.

2 Using the fine paintbrush, begin working from either the top or the bottom of the glass, painting a winding vine around the bowl and stem. To ensure that the paint does not smudge while you are working, allow one area to dry before beginning the next one.

Above right: The completed glasses
*Below left and right: Painting in the design
of the vines and leaves*

PAINTED PLATES

What a very bright and happy image these clowns create when painted on to a set of wall plaques! They make the perfect decoration for a child's room. Birthday cards, gift wrapping, toys and children's picture books are all good sources of inspiration for a project like this one.

MATERIALS
white wall plates
tracing paper
pencil
chinagraph pencil
ceramic paints: black, cherry red,
　　lavender, blue, orange, yellow
　　and green
ceramic varnish

INSTRUCTIONS

1 Draw or trace your chosen design on to tracing paper, then copy it on to a plate using the chinagraph pencil.

2 Take into account the round shape of the plate when you are drawing your design. You can make the feet follow the edge or the hands

appear to support the top edge, or have the clown doing a handstand. Whatever design you choose, always cover as much of the plate as possible.

3 Draw in the outline with a line of black ceramic paint, then paint in the main features, such as the clothes and hair. Colour the clothes very bright and busy, with plenty of spots, checks and patches.

4 Fill in the background with another busy pattern of circles, triangles or wavy lines painted in more bright contrasting colours.

5 Allow the paint to dry completely, then paint with a protective coat of ceramic varnish.

Sketching the design from a greeting card

Drawing the design on to the plate

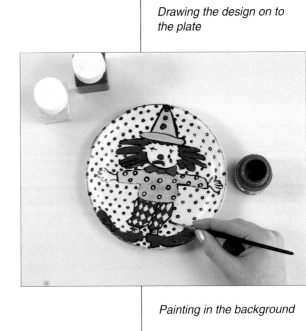

Painting in the background

Left: The completed plates

SUPER SCALES

A set of old scales becomes a stylish decorator item when it is painted in gold and black with a traditional design picked out in old gold.

MATERIALS
scrap paper
pencil
old kitchen scales
fine sandpaper
ceramic paints: gold and black
gold spray paint
3 cm paintbrush
fine paintbrush
newspaper

INSTRUCTIONS

1 Clean the scales thoroughly with soapy water to remove all the grease and grime, then sand down with the fine sandpaper.

2 Apply one coat of black paint with the 3 cm brush. Apply a second coat, if required, to completely cover the old finish. Leave to dry.

3 Choose an appropriate design from a book, a stencil design, wallpaper or fabric. Experiment with the design on paper until you are happy with the result.

4 Using the fine brush, paint the outline of the design in gold, then fill it in with more gold paint.

5 If the scales are to be ornamental only, spray the dish of the scales with gold paint. If you are going to use the scales for weighing food, it is better not to paint the dish, but to clean it up with a good metal scourer. Always use spray paints in a well-ventilated area and mask the surrounding area carefully with newspaper to protect it from any overspray.

Above: The completed scales
Right: Paint the scales with black ceramic paint
Far right: Paint in the design with gold ceramic paint

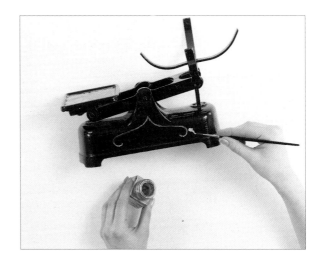

STRAWBERRY TRAY

What a charming notion! Decorate a simple pine tray with a pattern derived from your favourite china tea set. On the other hand, if you like this strawberry design, you can buy some china to match. Or you can use the techniques described here to paint a tray to match your own tea set.

Top: Tracing the design from the tea set
Above: Cutting out the stencil

MATERIALS

pine tray
tracing paper
pencil
masking tape
sheets of clear acetate for the stencils
coloured pencils in appropriate colours
fineline permanent marker pen
sharp craft knife
cutting board (optional)
sandpaper
lint-free cloth
acrylic paints in appropriate colours
    (quick-drying stencil paints are
    ideal)
small stencil brush
old saucer or plate for a palette
clear varnish
5 cm paintbrush

INSTRUCTIONS

1 Tape small pieces of tracing paper over the areas of the design you wish to use. Trace off the elements either singly, as single leaves and strawberries, or as groups.

2 Using your tracings, combine the elements into a pleasing design. Trace the new outline on to another sheet of tracing paper. It is a good idea at this stage to colour in your design with the coloured pencils so you can judge its effectiveness.

3 Transfer the design to several sheets of acetate (one for each colour), using the fineline pen.

4 You will need to make a separate stencil for each colour. To do this, cut out of each sheet the elements you wish to paint in a particular colour, using the craft knife. Take care when

cutting out to leave 'bridges' in the design such as down the spine of a leaf or between stalks and leaves.

5 Sand the tray all over with the sandpaper until it is quite smooth. Wipe away the sandings with the lint-free cloth.

6 Position the first stencil (in this case the green one) on a corner of the tray and tape it in place. Place a small amount of paint on the saucer or plate. Using the small stencil brush, paint in the green areas of the design using a dabbing motion. Take care not to load the brush with too much paint. Repeat the process for all the green areas on the tray. Allow the paint to dry completely.

7 With the clean stencil brush, paint in the next colour (red) in the same way as the green, then the white and finally the yellow. To avoid smudging, make sure each last colour is dry before you apply the next one.

8 To complete the tray, you can decorate around the sides and around the handles with small stencils.

9 When all the stencilling is complete and the paint is dry, apply a coat of clear varnish to all the surfaces.

Below: Painting the first colour
Bottom: Completing the painting of the stencil

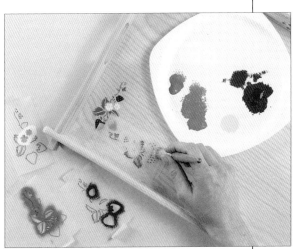

FOLK ART SHELF

This delightful little shelf, destined to house a collection of thimbles, has been painted with a number of traditional folk art motifs relating to sewing and quilting. It is an original design by Annette Johnson. Craft shops sell shelves like this in a raw form, in a kit, or assembled ready to paint.

MATERIALS

small timber shelf
fineline permanent marker pen
blue saral paper
stylus
kneadable eraser
burnt umber oil paint
antiquing liquid
lint-free cloth
round sable brush, size 2
flat brushes, sizes 4 and 6
pale cream and dusty blue paint for base coats
Deco Art Americana paints: French grey blue, snow white, uniform blue, cranberry wine, burnt umber, avocado, ebony black, blue haze, raw sienna, light cinnamon, dusty rose, lavender, neutral grey, slate grey. (You can use any folk art paints in similar colours that are suitable for painting on wood.)
spray gloss varnish
wet and dry sandpaper, 600 grade
normal sandpaper

INSTRUCTIONS

See the designs on the Pull Out Pattern Sheet.

PREPARATION

1 Base coat the shelf with four coats of pale cream, sanding well between each coat. Do not sand the final coat.

2 Trace the painting designs and transfer them to the positions shown on the shelf, using the stylus and blue saral paper. Blue saral paper is not as waxy as graphite paper and will not clog the nib of your pen as you draw over the design lines.

3 Outline all the tracing lines using the fineline pen. If you make a mistake, wet a small piece of the wet and dry sandpaper and gently rub the mistake away.

4 Let the ink dry for about one hour then remove all visible saral lines with the kneadable eraser.

PAINTING

1 This shelf is painted using washes, i.e. a mix of 80% water and 20% paint. Use the round brush, size 2 for this step. When all the washes have been completed, shade with the flat brush that fits best in the area you are shading. Shading is done with full-strength paint and only the water in your brush.

2 Mix French grey blue and snow white. Wash all hearts, dots and commas dividing each drawing, the ribbon on the one bonnet, the scissor handles, the fabric on the quilt, the ruching on the dress, the band on the dress collar, two buttons, the bow on the straw hat, two pin heads, the bottom half of the fan, and the lettering. Shade in uniform blue.

3 Mix cranberry wine and burnt umber. Wash the button, all the flowers, stripes on the large button, and the quilt fabric. Shade with the same mixture.

4 Mix avocado, ebony black and snow white. Wash all the leaves and quilt fabric. Shade with a mixture of avocado and blue haze.

5 With blue haze, wash the dilly bag and the feather on the pen. Shade with blue haze.

6 With raw sienna, wash the letter next to the pen, the straw hat, the pin box, the button, the ruler, the thimble, the calendar, the quilt fabric, the nib of the pen, and the ink label. Shade with light cinnamon.

7 With light cinnamon, wash the pen handle, the umbrella handle, the cotton spool ends, the boot heel and sole. Shade with burnt umber.

8 With dusty rose, wash the umbrella frills, the top section of the fan, the button, the quilt, the scallop part of the boot, the bow on the dilly bag. Shade with burnt umber.

9 Mix lavender and neutral grey. Wash the cotton on the spool, the quilt, a button, the bow on the fan, the pins, the umbrella and bows, the quilt edge. Shade with the same mix.

10 With uniform blue, wash the ink bottle and the back part of the boot. Shade with uniform blue.

11 With snow white, wash the dress and bonnet. Shade with slate grey. With slate grey, wash the scissor blades. Shade with ebony black. When all the painting is dry, reinforce with the fineline pen any lines painted over. Paint the shelf edges with a 1:1 mixture of cream and dusty blue.

12 Varnish the shelf all over when the paint is dry.

Give your shelf an antique finish before varnishing, if you wish.

Furniture Facelifts

Decorative painting can work miracles on furniture that has become a little 'tired' and worn. Whether you have a garage full of well-used chairs or are a devotee of jumble sales, consider the possibilities that painting opens up.

Before you begin, make sure that the piece of furniture is worth all your hard work. Check that the structure is basically sound – or that you can fix any problems without undue cost. Remember, rotting timber will not be made stronger with a lovely stencilled pattern.

Next, prepare your surface well. If it is already painted, you will need to remove the old paint layers with a good paint stripper. Fill any holes and sand the entire piece until it is quite smooth. If it is not painted, you should still make sure the surface is clean and free of wax or polish and that there are no holes or cracks.

Which style of painting you choose is up to you. Stencilling lends itself very well to furniture and it is remarkably simple to achieve a very good result. Freehand painting requires a little more effort but the results are very rewarding.

The charming cane chair opposite was quite solid but very drab until its facelift. First it was sprayed with a white aerosol paint, using three light coats to give a good covering. The roses were first drawn on with a soft pencil and then painted with acrylic paints. You will need to mix colours to get this range of shades, using the darker ones to give depth to the design and the lighter ones for highlights.

TOY CHEST

A battered pine chest can take on a new lease of life with this wonderful painted design of friendly animals. As a special touch, personalise your painted chest with the name of the owner. If you want to hand it down from generation to generation, paint in the family name and you have the makings of a family heirloom which will be loved by generations of children.

MATERIALS

pine chest
steel wool
mineral turpentine (white spirit)
sandpaper
soapy water
rag
tracing paper
pencil
transfer paper
stylus
black fineline permanent marker pen
masking tape
*acrylic paints in suitable colours,
    including black and white*
old saucer or plate for a palette
suitable paintbrushes
clear gloss varnish

Below: Transferring the design to the toy chest
Below right: Painting in the design
Right: The completed toy chest

INSTRUCTIONS

See the design on the Pull Out Pattern Sheet.

1 The surface of the chest should be absolutely clean if the paint is to adhere properly. If there is any wax on the wood, remove it by rubbing with the steel wool dipped in mineral turpentine (white spirit). Wipe off all the grime and rubbings with the rag dipped in soapy water.

2 When the wood is quite dry sand the chest all over, inside and out.

3 Trace the design from the Pattern Sheet on to tracing paper. You will need to adjust the size of the design to suit the size of your own toy chest. The simplest way to do this is on a photocopying machine. Using two elements of the design, say the smallest and the biggest, work out an appropriate enlargement to suit you. If you do not have access to a photocopier, use the grid method described on page 7 to enlarge the design.

4 When you have a drawing of the right size, tape it in position on the toy chest, using masking tape. Slip a sheet of transfer paper between the drawing and the wooden surface and go over all the outlines with the stylus, transferring them to the chest. On a wooden surface these markings may be quite faint so you will need to go over them with the pencil or the fineline pen.

5 Draw in the name in the space provided.

6 Using the old saucer or plate for your palette, mix up some paints with a little black or white to add tonal variation to the flat colours. Paint in the designs.

7 When the paint is completely dry, strengthen the outlines, whiskers and facial features by drawing over them with the fineline pen.

8 Paint one or two coats of clear gloss varnish over the whole chest to protect the painted design. You will also see how the colours come to life with a coat or two of varnish.

SPONGED CABINET

Transform an old cabinet, long past its prime, with a wonderful painted effect and new china handles painted to match. Before you begin working on your transformation, make sure that the cabinet is solid – don't waste your efforts on furniture that is about to fall apart.

MATERIALS

an old cabinet
newspaper
paint stripper
scraping tool
detergent
wood filler
sandpaper
wood primer
undercoat
5 cm paintbrush
water-based base colour (light colour)
water-based second colour (medium colour)
water-based third colour (darkest colour)
ceramic paint for the handles
natural sponge
plain white china handles
fine paintbrush

INSTRUCTIONS

1 You will first need to remove the old finish and for this step it is important to work in a well-ventilated room. Remove the old handles and spread plenty of newspaper on the floor. Use the paint stripper following the manufacturer's instructions.

2 Wash down the cabinet with a mild detergent-and-water solution. Fill any holes with wood filler.

3 When the cabinet is dry, sand it all over until it is quite smooth.

4 Apply a wood primer and then an undercoat, following the manufacturer's instructions. Allow the surface to dry between coats.

5 Apply the base coat (light colour) with the 5 cm paintbrush and allow it to dry.

6 Wet the sponge and squeeze out any excess water, leaving it just damp. Dip the sponge into the second paint colour, dabbing any excess paint off on some scrap paper. Dab the paint on. Do not cover the surface with this colour but leave plenty of gaps for the third colour.

7 After cleaning the sponge, apply the third colour in the same way, filling in the gaps and overlapping the sponging already in place.

8 While the cabinet is drying, you can decorate the new china handles with the ceramic paint and the fine paintbrush. Choose any design, such as flowers, leaves or ribbon garlands. If you need inspiration, china patterns on plates and cups are a good source of designs.

Right: Removing the old finish

Top: Sponging on the third colour
Above: Painting the new china handles
Right: The completed cabinet

MARBLED PLANT STAND

A good marbling effect can be quite difficult to achieve so it is a good idea to practise on a spare piece of timber until you are happy with the result.

MATERIALS

plain wooden pedestal
wood for practising on
primer and/or undercoat
black matt or low-sheen premium
    paint
white matt or low-sheen premium
    paint
scumble medium
mineral turpentine
paintbrushes, one small round, one
    6-8 cm and one fine artist's brush
soft cloth
stipple brush
clear varnish
brush for applying varnish

INSTRUCTIONS

1 Apply primer and/or undercoat following the manufacturer's instructions.

2 Paint the pedestal with the black matt or low-sheen premium paint. Allow to dry.

3 Mix a white glaze consisting of 20% white matt or low-sheen premium paint, 20% mineral turpentine and 60% scumble medium. Dab on this white glaze, using the 6-8 cm brush. Don't completely white out the black background, but allow some of it to show through.

4 While the white glaze is still wet, dab over it with the soft cloth, crumpled. This should soften any hard edges and spread the white glaze.

5 Continue to soften the glaze by working over it with a stipple brush and the soft cloth dipped in mineral turpentine.

6 Mix a little black glaze using the same proportions of paint, scumble medium and mineral turpentine as for the white glaze. Using this and the fine paintbrush, draw in some veins. Make them quite irregular and broken and soften any hard edges with the stipple brush.

7 Using the white glaze and the fine paintbrush, draw in some white veins and stipple as before.

8 When the paint is dry, apply a coat or two of clear varnish to give the glossy appearance of marble.

Above right: Painting the pedestal
Right: Applying the white glaze

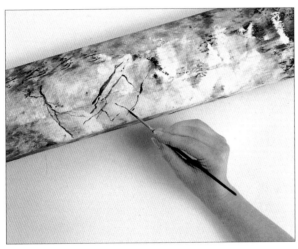

Top: Dabbing off some of the white glaze
Above: Painting in the veins
Right: The marbled plant stand

STENCILLED BEDROOM

Transform a dull
room into a little
girl's delight
with some very
inexpensive
touches. The
stencilled
bluebirds and
trailing bows are
repeated on the
walls, bed, chest of
drawers and even
give new life to an
old cane chair.

If you are really
enthusiastic, you
can stencil some
bed linen and
even floorboards
in the same
bluebird theme.

The same design has been used for all the stencilling, with adaptations to the basic design to suit the particular angle or surface where it is to be used. For example, the stencilled border that travels up the wall to the old chimney breast uses only the right-hand bird from the original design, with the upper wing omitted.

BED DRAPES

Add a touch of romance with these simple bed drapes, highlighted with bows and stencilling.

MATERIALS
water-based paint in white and sky blue
large brush
damp cotton cloth
electric drill
3 wall plugs
3 brass hooks
approximately 16 m white muslin
5 m of 2 cm wide peach satin ribbon
masking tape
white sewing thread
tracing paper
pencil
sheets of clear acetate for the stencil
fineline permanent marker pen
sharp craft knife
old saucer or plate for a palette
quick-drying stencil paints or acrylic paint in blue and peach
stencil brush

INSTRUCTIONS
See the design on the Pull Out Pattern Sheet.

1 Paint the wall with the white water-based paint. Allow to dry. Mix up a pale blue wash by diluting the sky blue water-based paint. Using the large brush, swish on the pale blue to give a soft streaky effect. If some parts are too strong, lighten them by lifting a little of the colour with the damp cloth while the paint is still wet. Allow the paint to dry thoroughly.

2 Find the centre point on the wall approximately 1.5 m above the bed. Drill and plug a hole at this point, then screw in a small brass hook.

3 Find the centre of the 16 m length of muslin. Gather the fabric gently at the centre and tie a bow of satin ribbon to hold the gathering in place. Leave the ends of the ribbon to trail down. Tie a second bow to the hook and then around the muslin to create a double bow with four trailing ends. Trim the ends at various lengths, cutting them at an angle.

4 Mark a point on either side of the bed, approximately 30 cm below the centre hook. Experiment to find the right point by gathering and draping the muslin. Drill and plug a hole at each of these points and insert the brass hooks.

Above right: Securing the muslin drape
Right: Stencilling the bluebird design

52

5 On the muslin, mark equal distances on either side of the centre where the drape finishes. As before, tie two satin bows at each of these points, attaching the muslin to the hooks. Remove the tape.

6 Hem the muslin at an appropriate point. You can have it ending just above floor level or have it mounded up luxuriously as shown on page 50.

7 Trace the individual bluebirds from the Pattern Sheet on to a sheet of acetate with the fineline pen. Cut out the stencil with the craft knife. Tape each one to the wall above the centre hook. Place a little paint on the old saucer or plate. Remove the muslin before you begin painting. Paint in the stencil design. Clean the stencils in water several times while you work as they become clogged very easily.

8 Make a separate stencil for the bow in the same way as for the bluebirds. Stencil the three birds with trailing ribbons around each of the side hooks and one more bluebird below each hook as shown. Always make sure the paint is dry when lifting and moving stencils to their next position.

9 When all the paint is dry, replace the muslin drape.

53

CANE CHAIR

This lovely old Lloyd Loom chair has been stencilled with bluebirds, but the wall stencil would have been too delicate for the texture of the chair so a stencil with more dramatic effect has been chosen.

Below: The completed cane chair
Right: Spraying the first stencil
Below right: Adding the second colour

MATERIALS

white cane chair
spray paint in white, blue and peach
tracing paper
pencil
3 sheets of clear acetate for the stencils
fineline permanent marker pen
sharp craft knife
paper for masking
masking tape

INSTRUCTIONS

See the design on the Pull Out Pattern Sheet.

1 First spray the chair all over with blue. Allow to dry. Do not attempt to cover the white background completely.

2 Trace the three stencil designs from the Pattern Sheet on to three pieces of acetate with the fineline pen. Cut out the stencils.

3 Tape the bow stencil on the centre back of the chair. Tape paper around the stencil to mask the rest of the chair. Spray the stencil in a peach colour. It is best to spray several light coats from about 30 cm away until the cane is well covered but not clogged with paint.

4 Tape one bluebird stencil on the left-hand side of the bow. Mask around it as before. Spray the stencil in white as for the bow. When the paint is dry, carefully remove the stencil. Paint the bluebird on the other side in the same way.

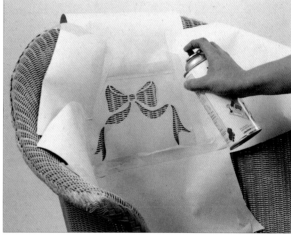

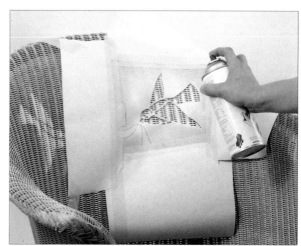

CHEST OF DRAWERS

MATERIALS
chest of drawers
tracing paper
pencil
sheets of clear acetate for the stencils
fineline permanent marker pen
sharp craft knife
paper for masking
masking tape
old saucer or plate for a palette
fast-drying stencil paints or acrylic
    paints in blue and peach
clear varnish

INSTRUCTIONS
See the designs on the Pull Out
Pattern Sheet.

1 If your chest of drawers is looking
a little battered, you will need to
give it a couple of coats of white,
water-based gloss paint before you
begin stencilling.

2 Trace the large bow from the
Pattern Sheet on to a piece of
acetate, using the fineline pen. For the
smaller bow, trace the design from the
Pattern Sheet on to tracing paper.
Sketch in another loop on the left-
hand side of the bow. Turn this bow
slightly so the ribbon tails hang vertically. Transfer the design to another
piece of acetate, using the fineline
pen. Mark in the position of the
bluebirds on both sides so you can
align them properly when you come
to paint them in. Cut out the stencils
using the craft knife. Make a bird
stencil in the same way. If you have
already made a stencil of which you
could use a part, simply mask off any
area you do not wish to use.

3 Mark the centre of each drawer.
Place a little paint in the old
saucer or plate. Position and paint the
stencils as shown in the photograph,
cleaning and flipping over the stencils
as necessary. Take care not to lift and
move the stencils until the paint is
completely dry to avoid smudging.

4 When all the stencilling is
complete, paint the chest with a
coat of clear varnish.

*This is another
well-used piece of
furniture that has
been given a new
lease of life. You
will need to adapt
the stencil used
for the bed drapes
for the smaller bow
on the second
drawer. The larger
bow is given on the
Pattern Sheet and
the bluebird is the
one on the right
above the bed
drapes.*

*Below left: Cutting out the
stencils
Below: Painting the stencil
on the drawers*

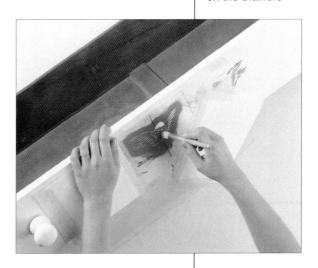

WALL BORDER

A dainty border is a pretty feature on most walls and especially those where there are interesting nooks and crannies to be emphasised. Border stencils, such as this one, look most effective along skirting boards, dado rails, below window ledges or along cornices.

MATERIALS
pencil
ruler
sheets of clear acetate for the stencils
fineline permanent marker pen
sharp craft knife
masking tape
old saucer or plate for a palette
fast-drying stencil paint or acrylic
   paint in peach, terracotta and blue
stencil brush

INSTRUCTIONS
See the design on the Pull Out Pattern Sheet.

1 Trace the bluebirds from the Pattern Sheet on to the acetate with the fineline pen. Trace part of the peach bows, using a dotted line, to help you position the design later on. Mark the top and side lines to use as registration marks for lining up your design accurately. Cut out the bluebird stencil with the sharp knife. Make a separate stencil for the bows in the same way, marking the top and sides as before.

2 Rule a faint horizontal line in pencil on the wall where you wish the top of the stencil to fall. Line up the top mark on the stencil with the pencil line on the wall. Tape the stencil in place. Place a small amount of peach paint on the saucer. Paint in the peach bows with a dabbing motion. Leave to dry.

3 Lift off the bow stencil and tape it in the next position, using the registration marks you have drawn. Continue until you have finished the entire border of bows. Clean your stencil frequently to avoid it becoming clogged with paint.

4 When the paint is nearly dry, dab on some terracotta colour with a clean brush at the points where the ribbons twist and overlap to give a three-dimensional effect.

5 Work along the border with the bluebird stencil and blue paint in the same way as for the bows, matching registration marks and the dotted lines. Clean the stencil frequently as you work.

Left: Use the wall border to accentuate interesting corners

RIBBON BOWS

MATERIALS

sheet of clear acetate for the stencil
fineline permanent marker pen
sharp craft knife
pencil
masking tape
old saucer or plate for a palette
fast-drying stencil paint or acrylic
  paint in peach and terracotta
stencil brush

INSTRUCTIONS

See the design on the Pull Out
Pattern Sheet.

1 Trace the stencil design from the
  Pattern Sheet on to the acetate
with the fineline pen. Cut it out.

2 Mark on the wall the position of
  the top of the picture. Remove the
picture. Tape the stencil, centred
above the picture, so that the ends of
the bow trail down behind it.

3 Place a little peach paint in the
  saucer. Paint in the design.

4 When the paint is nearly dry, dab
  on some terracotta colour with a
clean brush. Do this where the

ribbons twist and overlap to give a
three-dimensional effect. Blend the
terracotta colour into the peach so
there are no sudden colour changes.

Above: The ribbon bow
Left: Stencilling the peach colour

FLORENTINE HALLWAY

This is an ideal situation for a stencilled 'wallpaper' effect. Paint the wall below the dado rail in a colour to complement the stencilling.

WALL PATTERN

MATERIALS
long ruler
pencil
sheets of clear acetate for the stencils
fineline permanent marker pen
sharp craft knife
string and weight for a plumb line
masking tape
old saucer or plate for a palette
fast-drying stencil paint
stencil brush

INSTRUCTIONS

1 Work out how far apart you wish to have the motifs – approximately 9 cm apart vertically and 7.5 cm apart horizontally looks good. For tight corners, you will need only one or two motifs on the stencil, but it will obviously speed up your work in the larger areas to have six or eight motifs on the stencil. Consider cutting two stencils – a small and a large one.

2 Trace the motif from this page on to the acetate with the fineline pen. Draw in horizontal and vertical registration lines to help you align the stencils. Draw in with dotted lines the other motif outlines. Cut out the stencils with the craft knife.

3 Find the centre of the wall and, using the plumb line and a long ruler, lightly mark a vertical pencil line from the ceiling down to the dado rail.

4 Tape the stencil to the wall with masking tape, lining up the first vertical row of motifs with the pencil line on the wall and placing the first motif about 5 cm from the ceiling. Check that this gives you sufficient room (approximately 12 cm) above the dado rail for the border. You may need to adjust the spacing slightly.

5 Place a little paint in the saucer or plate and begin painting in the stencil with a dabbing motion to give a soft grainy texture. If you are using a small two-motif stencil, overlap the lower one you have just painted with the upper one on the next section to space the rows correctly.

6 When the paint is dry, work the next vertical row of stencils, matching up the dotted lines with the painted motifs. Continue stencilling, adjusting the spacing slightly to allow for awkward corners or uneven rows. Stencil up to 13 cm of the mirror's edge. If there are any large gaps near the curved surface, it is best to leave these until you have painted the border and then add in another motif where necessary.

Right: Cutting out the stencil
Far right: The stencilled hallway and table

59

Follow these steps to ensure that the border follows exactly the curve of the mirror or table.

HALL TABLE

MATERIALS
tracing paper
large sheet of white paper
pencil
sheets of clear acetate for the stencils
fineline permanent marker pen
scissors
sharp craft knife
masking tape
old saucer or plate for a palette
fast-drying stencil paints or acrylic
  paints in white and blue
stencil brush
kitchen paper
clear varnish

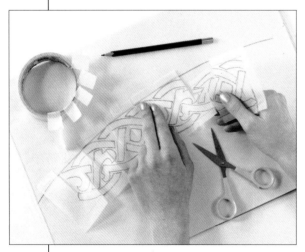

Above right: Cutting the curved tracings
Right: Stencilling in the first colour on the table

INSTRUCTIONS
See the design on the Pull Out Pattern Sheet.

1 Trace the exact curve of the table on to the large sheet of white paper.

2 Trace the design from the Pattern Sheet on to sheets of tracing paper. Cut slits alternately in the top and bottom of these tracings so that they can bend. Tape the border design over the curved traced line on the white paper, bending it to fit.

3 Lay the acetate over the top of the design on the curved line and trace in the adapted design with the fineline pen, extending and shortening lines as necessary. Cut one stencil for each colour to be used, based on this adapted design. Mark dotted registration lines and the curved line of the table's edge on both stencils.

4 Tape the 'white' stencil in place and dab in the white paint to make a soft grainy effect. Leave to dry before removing the stencil.

5 Tape the 'blue' stencil in place, matching dotted lines and registration marks. Dab in the blue colour, using very little paint on an almost dry brush (remove excess paint with the kitchen paper) to give the subtle mottled finish. Leave to dry before removing the stencil.

6 Paint the table top with a coat of clear varnish.

MIRROR BORDER

1 Trace the design from the Pattern Sheet on to the acetate with the fineline pen. Cut the bottom edge of the stencil so it will run along the dado rail and make the stencilling job much easier. Tape the stencil in place and paint as for the table border.

2 When you reach a corner, lay a piece of masking tape across the corner at 45° to mitre the corner. Paint up to the tape on both stencils.

3 Make a curved stencil in the same way as for the table top. Paint in the curved mirror frame in the same way and then paint in the straight sides, mitring the corners at the bottom to match up with the rest of the border.

Top: The mirror border
Above: Stencilling in the second colour on the table

STENCILLED BATHROOM

Is your bathroom quite functional but a bit drab? This wall stencil can be reduced to one-fifth of its size to decorate a pile of fluffy towels or the pretty flounce around the washbasin.

WALL BORDER

MATERIALS
water-based interior house paints in
    white and yellow
brush or roller
damp natural sponge
pencil
ruler
old plates or saucers for palettes
sheets of clear acetate for the stencils
fineline permanent marker pen
sharp craft knife
cutting board (optional)
masking tape
fast-drying stencil paints or acrylic
    paints in yellow, dark pink and
    green
small sponges

INSTRUCTIONS
See the stencil design on the Pull Out Pattern Sheet.

1 Paint the walls white and then, using the large damp sponge dipped in the yellow interior paint, dab paint on to the wall in an even manner. Take care not to have too much paint on the sponge.

2 Mark a faint pencil line around the wall where you wish to stencil.

3 Make two stencils – one for the flowers and one for the leaves. Trace the flowers from the Pattern Sheet on to one sheet of acetate with the fineline pen, drawing in the leaves with dotted lines. Cut out the flowers. Make a second stencil for the leaves, marking in the flowers with dotted lines. Cut out the leaves.

4 Tape the flower stencil in position on the pencil line. Using a small sponge and the yellow stencil paint, dab in the colour around the outside of the flowers. Dab in the pink colour at the flower centres, blending the pink with the yellow. Stencil the flowers all around the wall in this way, linking the stencils by matching up the dotted lines.

5 In the saucers or plates, mix up several shades of green, from lime to emerald, by combining the yellow and green acrylic paints in different proportions. Tape the leaf stencil in place at the first position, matching the dotted lines to the flower outlines. Dab in the green, varying the shades of green over the design to add interest. Apply the colour lightly to blend in with the sponged effect on the wall.

Left: Sponging the walls with yellow
Above right: The stencilled bathroom
Right: Stencilling in the first colour
Far right: Stencilling in the second colour

To set off your stylish new bathroom, trim a set of towels with a stencilled fabric strip to match the walls. Highlight the colours of the stencilling with bands of satin ribbon.

TOWEL

MATERIALS
towel
strip of smooth white cotton fabric, approximately 20 cm wide x width of the towel
pencil
ruler
sheets of clear acetate for the stencils
fineline permanent marker pen
sharp craft knife
cutting board (optional)
masking tape
paper or fabric for masking
fabric paints in yellow, dark pink and green
old plate or saucer for a palette
stencil brush
satin ribbon in two colours, twice as long as the towel is wide plus 4 cm
matching sewing thread

INSTRUCTIONS
See the designs on the Pull Out Pattern Sheet.

Right: The stencilled towels and bathmat, made in the same way as the towels, using the larger stencil

1 Make two stencils – one for the flowers and one for the leaves. Trace the flowers from the Pattern Sheet, drawing in the leaves with dotted lines. Draw in a horizontal line at the top and bottom for registration lines. Cut out the flowers. Make a stencil in the same way for the leaves, drawing in the flowers with dotted lines.

2 Mask your work area with paper or fabric. Tape the cotton fabric strip to the masking.

3 With the ruler and pencil, draw in a faint horizontal line 5 cm from the top edge to match up with the line on the stencil.

4 Tape the leaves stencil on top of the fabric strip, matching lines. Paint in the leaves in a mixture of yellow and green. Allow the paint to dry before lifting the stencil and taping it in its new position, matching dotted lines and registration marks. Complete the border of leaves in this way.

5 Using the flower stencil and working in the same way as for the leaves, paint the outside of the flowers in yellow. For the flower centres, blend in dark pink paint. Allow to dry. Fix the paints following the manufacturer's instructions.

6 Trim the stencilled strip along the pencil lines. Stitch the stencilled strip along the width of the towel, turning under the raw edges at both ends and stitching them down.

7 Pin a length of satin ribbon over the raw edges of the fabric strip and stitch it in place. Stitch another length of ribbon parallel to the first.

Ray Bradley

MACMILLAN
EDUCATION

Acknowledgements

The author and publishers wish to thank the following for permission to reproduce their photographs:

AEB, p.14
Benson, p.21
Burroughs, p.14
British Telecommunication PLC, p.34
Hewlett Packard, pp 10, 11, 20, 21, 23, 25, 26, 43
ICL, pp.58, 59
LEB, p.16
Microvitec, p.19
Moniter Press Features Ltd, p.78
Popperfoto Ltd, p.73
Rainbird Software Ltd, p.60
Science Photo Library, pp.10, 12 Dick Luria, 11, 55 Jerry Mason, Lawrence Midgate, 23 David Parker, 24 Martin Dohrn, 25 John Heseltine, 58 Peter Aprahamian, Paul Shambroom, 72 Tom McHugh, Hank Morgan, 73 Tom McHugh, 74 Hank Morgan.

The publishers have made every effort to trace the copyright holders, but if they have inadvertently overlooked any, they will be pleased to make the necessary arrangements at the first opportunity.

First published 1987

Published by
MACMILLAN EDUCATION LTD
Houndmills, Basingstoke, Hampshire RG21 2XS
and London

Companies and representatives
throughout the world

Designed, illustrated and typeset by
The Pen and Ink Book Co Ltd

Produced by AMR for
Macmillan Education Ltd

Printed in Hong Kong

British Library Cataloguing in Publication Data
Bradley, Ray
Computer Awareness.
1. Electronic data processing
I. Title II. Series
004   QA76
ISBN 0-333-43771-3

Contents

Introduction

This book forms part of a Macmillan series designed for use by a wide range of students in school and further education, to provide practice in the development of core skills and knowledge in a variety of essential areas.

In particular, the series aims to ensure competence in core skills so that potential employees – school and college leavers – actually master the basic skills required by employers. Many of the skills included in the series are also needed in everyday life.

The approach taken is to present information in clear and carefully controlled steps and to provide numerous straightforward questions and tasks designed to test skills and explore the information presented.

The books are suitable for use not only with those pupils and students normally expected to take GCSE examinations, but also with those at all levels of ability, including students on pre-vocational courses such as CPVE and RSA Vocational Preparation. Each book is based upon the syllabus of the basic skills tests of the Associated Examining Board (Stag Hill House, Guildford, Surrey GU2 5XJ).

The series does not provide a framework for GCSE courses, but the books can be used in connection with a recognised public examination. They can also be used to provide practice in the core competences in the curriculum for the 14 – 19 age group.

Using this Book

In most sections you will find that Tasks and Questions have been set. When working through do not skip these tasks and questions. They are designed to help you test your understanding of the work just covered.

It is essential that you get as much practical experience using computers as you can. It is not enough just to read this book, real understanding of computers can only come by using them as often as possible.

Before reading other sections you will need to understand a little *computer jargon*. This is the name given to the words that are used to describe basic things about computers.

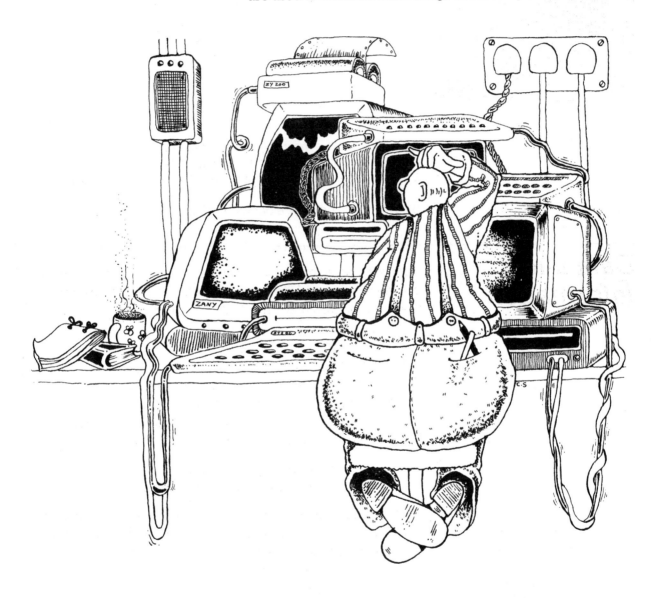

Basic Computer Jargon

Hardware

Hardware is the name given to the parts that make up a computer system. For example, the keyboard, disk drives and printers. It is important to realise that every piece of equipment, even things like the printer paper is hardware.

Software

When a computer does many wonderful things it is following a *set of instructions* called a *program*. (Note the spelling of the word!) Without a program, the computer system is like a record player without any records, i.e. not very useful. *Software* is the name given to the programs that control the hardware of a computer system. Without any software inside the machine, computers would be extremely difficult to use. Examples of software are spelling checkers, accounting systems, computer games and many many others.

Questions

1   Explain what is meant by the term hardware. Give three examples of hardware in a computer system.
2   What is meant by computer software? Give three examples of software.
3   What is the difference between software and programs?

Data and information

Data is the name given to the numbers, letters and symbols that are the raw material fed into a computer system. For example, the following data may be put into a computer.

21   28   34   12

When looking at data it is just a series of numbers or letters. The above set of numbers would be meaningless in themselves. However, suppose you were told that they correspond to dishes on the menu of a particular Chinese Take-Away. We might then find out that we have ordered:

king prawns, sweet and sour pork,
special fried rice and chop suey.

The numbers now have meaning. When meaning is applied to data it becomes *information*. Often the terms information and data are more loosely used in computing to mean the same thing.

User

This is the name given to the person who uses the computer. Throughout your course you will be a *computer user*.

Questions

1   Explain the difference between data and information.
2   What is a user?

What is a Computer?

As we are going to be doing a lot with computer systems it is useful to have a simple model to describe what a computer system is. Diagram A shows a picture of our simple model. Any computer system, no matter how complicated it looks, can be broken down into main sections. Diagram A shows the three main sections, these are *input, processing* and *output*.

The input is simply the information that you are going to feed into the system. The processing is what happens to the information that you have fed in. Finally, the output is what comes out after the processing has taken place.

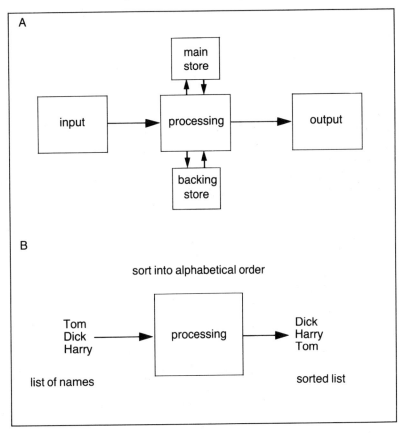

As an example, the input to a system could be a list of names, the processing could be sorting these names into alphabetical order, and the output would then be a new list of the names in alphabetical order. This simple example of *data processing* is shown in Diagram B.

1   Write down the input, processing and output that could be expected in the following systems:
    a) Doing some homework.
    b) A speak-your-weight machine.
    c) Playing a pop music record.

Questions

2   What is meant by the term data processing?
3   Explain the terms input, processing and output.

7

Why We Need Memory

A computer must follow a set of instructions called a program if it is to work on any particular task. For example, if a computer is programmed to carry out electricity billing, then a set of instructions which tell the computer what to do must be stored somewhere. The electricity billing program would be stored in the *short-term store* which is known as the *immediate access store,* or *main store.* This store is also shown in Diagram A.

Computers can be used to do an enormous variety of tasks, but the only programs that the computer needs at any one time are the ones that tell it how to do the current job. All the other programs can be stored away until they are needed. We therefore need a *long-term store.* This long-term store is called a *backing store* or *secondary store* and is again shown in Diagram A.

Computer and manual methods

The above processes are really quite simple and can be compared with manual operations or tasks done by hand. The diagram below shows a man sitting at a desk in his office.

There are two trays on the desk, an in tray, and an out tray. The man has a pencil and notebook and has access to a filing cabinet. We can now make a comparison between the computer system and the manual system to enable us to understand the computer system much more easily.

	Manual system	Computer system
Input	In tray	Keyboard etc.
Processor	A person's brain, pencil and paper.	Processing unit
Output	Out tray	Printer etc.
Immediate access store	A person's brain or notepad	Main store.
Backing store	Filing cabinet	Disk or tape.

If the computer is able to do all the above processes we can see that a computer is an *electronic machine* for *automatic data processing*. Throughout your course you will need to compare manual systems with computerised systems. Sometimes the computer system has no advantage over the manual system. In these cases, it would be silly to computerise. It is important that you can recognise this and also realise that there may be disadvantages in using computers. One of the main aims of this course is to show you the uses and limitations of computers in modern life.

Questions

1 Why do computers need memory?
2 Why do computers have both immediate access store and backing store?
3 What is normally stored inside the computer's memory?

Tasks

4 List the stages that would be necessary in a manual system for the following operations to be carried out:
   a) Paying a bill in a shop with a cheque.
   b) Checking the spelling in an English essay.
   c) Making a cup of tea.
5 The input, processor, output, immediate access store and backing store has been written down for drawing a picture:

Input ....Paper, coloured pencils, ideas for picture.

Processor ....Brain

Output..Finished picture

Immediate access store.........................Brain and possibly rough paper or notepad etc.

Backing store...Desk drawer where picture is kept (or even frame on the wall!)

Now choose at least two from the following list and write down your own ideas for input, processor etc.
   a) Building a model car.
   b) Making a pair of curtains.
   c) Repairing a puncture on a cycle.
   d) Marking a multiple choice maths test.

Types of Computer

The range of different types of computer available is enormous, but we can divide this range into only three major sections. These are *microcomputers, minicomputers* and *mainframe computers*. Each type is briefly described below.

Microcomputer

This type of computer is built around an electronic chip called a *microprocessor*. This is where the term microcomputer comes from. These computers tend to be very small compared with minis and mainframes. They are the types of computer that are found in the home, in small businesses and in schools. The price of microcomputers can vary from as little as £40 to as much as £10,000 for a sophisticated system. a typical microcompter is shown in Photograph A.

Minicomputers

These machines are more powerful and expensive than microcomputers. They are usually found in medium or large size businesses. They can handle large amounts of data and could cost up to several hundred thousand pounds. A typical minicomputer system is shown in Photograph B. It is also possible to have lots of extra equipment such as several disk drives and printers. Also, several people can often use the same computer at the same time by sitting down at different keyboards attached to the mini.

A

B

Mainframe computers

These are the largest computers and are very expensive, often costing as much as several million pounds. They are found only in the largest of organisations such as Government departments, Universities and very large businesses. However, many businesses have installed the smaller types of mainframe computer. A typical mainframe is shown in Photograph C.

C

D

The largest of mainframe computers are called *supercomputers*. These are fantastically powerful and are used for the most complex of tasks such as forecasting the weather, where millions of complex calculations must be carried out in seconds. A supercomputer is shown in Photograph D.

Questions

1 What are the names given to the three main types of computers?
2 Give a typical place or situation where each of the following might be found.
   a) microcomputer,
   b) minicomputer,
   c) mainframe computer.
3 Which type of computer would you recommend for the following?
   a) Controlling a small robot.
   b) Helping the police to investigate criminal records.

E
Many different computers being used in an office

Data Capture

Choosing the best method of entering data into a computer system is an important part of understanding computers and their uses. There are many ways of entering data and some of them will now be considered.

Input peripherals

A *peripheral* is the name given to a piece of hardware that is connected to the computer. Typical examples would be disk drives and printers. If a peripheral is used to input data into the computer system then it is called an *input peripheral*.

Questions

1 What is meant by the term data capture?
2 What is a peripheral?
3 Name two different types of peripheral that are used to input data into computer systems.

Manual data entry – the keyboard

Data entry by hand must always be prone to human error. However, manual data entry is necessary and important. The most common means of entering data manually into the computer is via the keyboard. A standard QWERTYUIOP keyboard is shown in Photograph A. It is called a QWERTYUIOP keyboard because of the layout of the top row of letters. Entry of data via the keyboard is very slow compared to other methods, even with an expert typist.

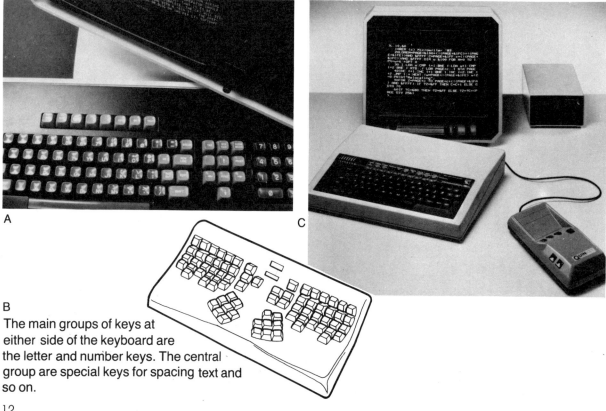

A

B
The main groups of keys at either side of the keyboard are the letter and number keys. The central group are special keys for spacing text and so on.

C

12

There are other types of keyboard which can improve the speeds at which the typist can type. An example of a non-standard keyboard is shown in Diagram B. Typing at the speed of speech is possible with these new keyboards. Another type of keyboard called the QUINKEY is shown in Photograph C. It is claimed that a non-specialist typist can be typing quickly after only a few hours of using this special type of keyboard.

Anybody can make an error when they enter data. If errors get into the computer system the results could be disastrous. We have all heard of the £1,000.000 electricity bill, or a final demand for £0.00! Various ways of detecting these errors have been thought up. One method which is used for keyboard data entry is called *verification*.

Verification

Verification is straightforward: one person types the data into the computer system where it is stored in a suitable way. At some later time a different person types in *the same data* again. The computer system then checks what is being typed in and *verifies* it to see if it is the same as the original data. If it is not, then the error will be brought to the attention of the keyboard operator so that appropriate action may be taken. Verification is also used in many automatic data entry systems.

Task

1   If you have a word processor this task will be much easier. Get a friend to time you for one minute. Type in some information (copy it out of this book if you like). After the minute is up, count up how many words you typed in. This is your typing speed in words per minute. How many mistakes did you make?

Questions

2   Why is it important to check that errors in data do not get into the computer system?
3   What type of error does verification detect?
4   How could you verify that two people had copied each other's work?
5   Is it possible to detect faulty data once it has been entered into the computer system?

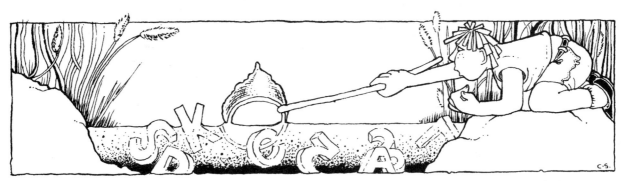

Automatic Data Entry

Manual data entry methods are very slow indeed compared with automatic methods. There are a variety of ways of entering data into the system automatically. However, they all have one thing in common. The data is *machine readable*. This means that it can be read by a machine.

MICR

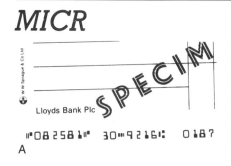

A

MICR means *Magnetic Ink Character Recognition*. Slightly strange shaped characters written with special ink are magnetised as they are being fed through a machine called a Magnetic Ink Character Reader. This is a method of data capture that is popular with the banks. Most people will be familiar with these special characters as they are printed on the bottom of cheques. An example is shown in Photograph A.

A MICR reader is shown in Photograph B.

When the cheques arrive at the clearing bank, the amount of the cheque is also written on the bottom using a machine that writes this information in special magnetic ink. When read into the MICR reader, the information about bank account, sorting code (a special code for each branch of the banks), the account number, and amount paid can be fed into the computer very quickly so that the day's transactions can be worked out automatically.

B

Mark sense readers

This is a system where marks can be made on a special form with an HB pencil. The form can then be fed into the *mark sense reader* and the marks that have been made are *sensed* by the machine. An example of this special type of form is shown in Photograph C.

C

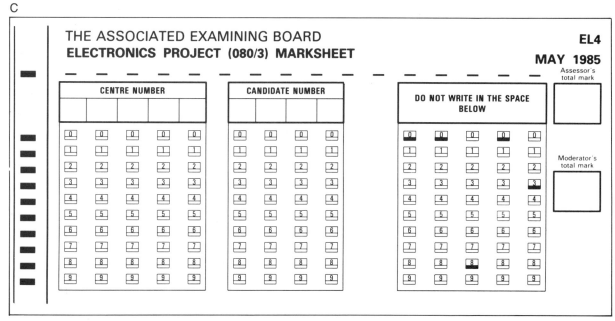

The particular form shown in Photograph C is for marking an electronics project examination. A mark is made with a pencil in the appropriate box. The forms are then fed into the mark sense reader which feeds data automatically into the computer system.

Questions

1 Why is it not necessary to have the name of the bank or the name of the person's account written on a cheque in special ink? Why is it not necessary to have the date written in special ink?
2 Some electricity boards are now using mark sense cards filled in by the meter reader. What advantages do you think that this has over the old system where the numbers had to be written down in a book and then typed into the computer? Are there any disadvantages for anybody?

Key-to-disk machines

Mainframe and large minicomputers often do many jobs at the same time. It would be inefficient if the computer had only to deal with the very slow process of people typing in data using a keyboard. Therefore, special machines called *key-to-disk* (keyboard to disk) *encoders* are often used. A typical key-to-disk machine is shown in diagram D.

The people typing in data at the keyboard type it into a machine which transfers the data onto magnetic disk. The disk can then be used at a later time to transfer the data into the computer system at a much higher speed. (Many thousands of times faster than typing it in.) Also, errors can be detected when the data is entered by means of verification. (see page 13.)

Key-to-tape machines

These are basically the same as the key-to-disk machines. The only difference being that the data is put onto magnetic tape instead of a disk.

15

Source documents

When data is to be entered into the computer it needs to be done efficiently. To help make data entry more efficient special forms called *source documents* are often used. Photograph E shows a typical source document. Source documents can be used by typists to enter data manually, or be used to read data directly into the computer.

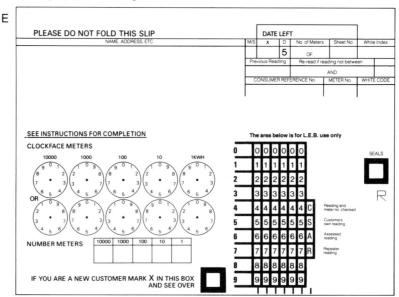

The source document shown in Photograph E contains characters that can be read by humans. They are therefore called *human readable characters*. In Photograph C, we saw a source document with characters that were machine readable. At the bottom of a cheque, the MICR characters are both human and machine readable.

Sometime it is useful to have a document which can be entered into the computer system again. For example, a computer might produce an electricity billing form to send to customers. When the bill is taken to the shop to be paid, the customer hands over the source document containing all the information such as address, meter readings and account number etc. After being fed into a special machine at the shop which is connected to the main computer system, the information on the document is used to inform the main computer that the bill has been paid. The customer may also retain part of the source document as a receipt.

Documents which are produced by a computer system, and then have more data added to them before being fed back into the computer system at a later date are called *turnaround documents*. The electricity billing example above is an example of a turnaround document.

Questions

1. Explain the terms MICR, mark sense, key-to-disk.
2. What is meant by the term source document?
3. Why is it necessary to have well designed source/turnaround documents?

Data Validation

When data has been entered into the computer system, it is often necessary to carry out some checks to see if it is sensible. We have already seen that verification is used to eliminate most of the typing errors, but it is still possible for incorrect data to get through the verification stage. This is because the data may have been correctly typed in, but incorrectly written in the first place. Again, the meter reading would be a good example.

Suppose Mr Potter has his electricity meter read and it happens to be:

$$0 \quad 2 \quad 3 \quad 9 \quad 7$$

Now this number is entered into the computer system and used to work out how much money he owes.

Now the next time his meter is read it might be:

$$0 \quad 2 \quad 5 \quad 4 \quad 3$$

Suppose that the meter person makes a mistake and enters the number:

$$0 \quad 2 \quad 3 \quad 4 \quad 3$$

This would be the number that is entered on the source document. Now when this number is typed in, the data entry staff type it faithfully. Similarly, when the data is again typed in by another person it is faithfully typed in and verified as correct. The error has not been detected!

However, when the computer comes to work out the bill it has to take away the old meter reading from the last one to find out how many units have been used. The sum is as follows:

$$0 \quad 2 \quad 3 \quad 4 \quad 3 - 0 \quad 2 \quad 3 \quad 9 \quad 7 = -5 \quad 4$$

This means that Mr Potter has not only used no electricity, but put some back into his meter! This is obviously impossible and therefore a mistake has been made. This data is not valid. The process where the computer is used to check the data once it has been entered correctly is called *data validation*.

Data validation is basically a check to see if data is within a sensible range. For example, if the weight of a person was typed in as 300 stone, then this is unlikely to be true. A sensible program may have a polite message on the screen saying that this is unlikely and please recheck before entering again.

You should be able to see that even if verification and validation have been carried out correctly, it is still possible to get wrong data into the computer system. This is not usually the computer's fault, but is human error. This also explains how it is still possible for a computer to send out an electricity bill for £1,000,000. However, it would be easy to get the computer to look at the last two or three bills and to generate an error message if the latest bill was drastically different from the others.

1 Choose a set of meter readings in the above system that would be drastically wrong, but still get through the verification and our simple validation checks.

2 What is meant by data validation?
3 Choose a sensible maximum value that could be used as a data validation check in the following cases:
   a) The age of pupils in a secondary school.
   b) The height of members of the police force.
   c) The weight of members of a slimming club.
4 Sometimes, even after data has been *verified* and *validated*, it can still be wrong when entered into a computer system. Give an example of where this could happen.

Output Peripherals

There are a variety of ways in which data can be obtained from a computer. The best method depends on factors such as the type of computer system, the type of output, (e.g. pictures or text, colour or black and white etc.), or whether the data is needed for a long time or a short time. That is, do you want to take a paper copy home or simply look at it on the screen for a few seconds?

If a permanent record of the data is needed that can be read by humans then it is likely that a *print-out* would be needed. This is referred to as *hard copy*. Often the data is only needed for a short space of time: for example, you may wish to find out the time of a television programme for this evening. In this case, a message on a TV screen would be quite adequate. This is called *soft copy*. Sometimes the data from a computer system only needs to be fed back into the computer system at a later date. In this case a disk or tape would be a more appropriate form of output.

1 Give some examples of data that would only need to be looked at for a few seconds on a computer screen.
2 Give some examples of data that would be best printed out on paper.
3 What is meant by the term hard copy?
4 What is meant by the term soft copy?

The VDU

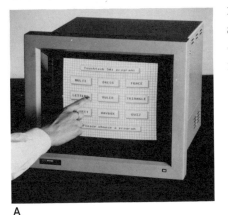

A

A VDU is a *visual display unit*. It is a TV-type screen but of a much higher quality. Higher quality screens are used so that small text may be more easily read on the screen, and good quality graphics pictures can be displayed. Both colour and monochrome (single colour) VDUs are available and some, especially designed for word processing, are coloured green or amber.

The screens come in a variety of sizes from domestic TV sizes up to very large screens used for Computer Aided Design. Some VDUs are touch sensitive. This means you can make things happen by touching your finger on the screen. This is shown in Photograph A.

Printers

Printers are the devices most commonly used for hard copy. There are many different types of printer but the main differences between each type is in the quality of print, speed of operation, and cost. Some types of printer are also able to produce pictures in colour or black and white.

Dot matrix

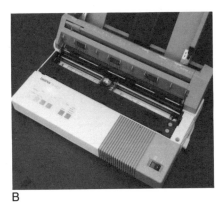

B

The most versatile and inexpensive form of printer is a *dot matrix printer* and one is shown in Photograph B.

The dot matrix printer forms characters from tiny dots. It has a versatile character set and can do double height characters, italics, bold, subscript, etc. as well as producing pictures. Although quite acceptable, the output from a dot matrix printer is not considered to be of a quality good enough for use in businesses where professional quality typewriters have been used for a long time.

```
Typical output from a
dot matrix printer.
```

C

Daisy wheel printers

D

If you are not interested in pictures, but require very high quality printing for letters to be sent to customers in a business then a *daisy wheel* printer would be more satisfactory. The printer uses a device to produce letters which looks like the petals on a daisy. This is why it is called a daisy wheel printer. A typical daisy wheel printer is shown in Photograph D, and the hard copy it produces is shown in E.

```
Typical output from a
daisy wheel printer.
```

E

Both types of printer are suitable for microcomputers where a low volume of output is required. Daisy wheel and dot matrix printers are very slow compared to the fast printers we are now going to consider. Typical speeds of a dot matrix printer might be 80 to 160 characters per second. This may sound very fast indeed, but it is far too slow when very large volumes of output such as rates bills or telephone bills are to be produced.

Questions

1 What is meant by a VDU, and why is it better than a TV for use with computer systems?
2 Why are different types of printer needed?
3 What are the main differences between the output produced by a dot matrix printer and a daisy wheel printer?
4 Why would a dot matrix printer be unsuitable for printing out 100 000 rates demands for a local council office?
5 Which printer would you suggest is used for the application given in question 4?

Higher speed printers

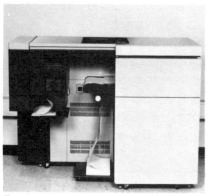

F

G

A line printer is the most common form of printer found on mini and mainframe computers. Its name comes from the fact that a whole line of text is produced in one go in about the time taken for a dot matrix printer to print a single character! A typical line printer is shown in Photograph F.

Other forms of very fast printer are being developed to replace the line printer. One of these newer types of printer is called a *laser printer*. A laser beam is used to form the image one page at a time. Due to the fact that a page is formed at once these types of printer are often called *page printers*. Some of the very expensive laser printers are extremely fast and also have the advantage that they can produce photographic quality pictures.

Much smaller less expensive laser printers are available which are suitable for connection to microcomputer systems. Such a system is extremely useful when used in conjunction with software packages such as a wordprocessor, a data base and drawing programs. These systems can be used by small businesses to produce their own highly professionly publications. An example of such a system is shown in Photograph G.

Task

Choose a suitable type of printer for each of the following applications:

a) Writing a letter to a friend.
b) Writing a business letter.
c) Printing 100 000 bills.
d) Listing a program.
e) Good quality pictures for a school magazine.
f) A simple map to tell your friend how to get to a party.

Other Forms of Hard Copy

There are many cases where high quality drawings are required. Examples might be architects plans or an engineering drawing. Although dot matrix printers could produce a poor quality copy, and laser printers could produce a high quality copy, they would both produce hard copy much too small to be of any use. Much bigger high quality diagrams can be produced on devices called *plotters*. Some of the types of plotter can be seen in Photograph A and Photograph B.

Photograph A shows what is called a *flatbed plotter*. This is simply because the plotter lies flat. Flatbed plotters vary in size and price from a simple one that could be connected to a micro, but whose output may be limited to about A4 size, to very large and expensive systems whose output can be enormous. Photograph B shows a variation of the plotters called a *drum plotter*. This type of plotter produces the pictures by rotating the paper on a drum.

Both the flatbed and drum plotters are capable of drawing diagrams in colour. This is done by putting different coloured pens into the machine. Often, the machine can choose up to ten different colours without the need for the operator to change any of the pens.

A

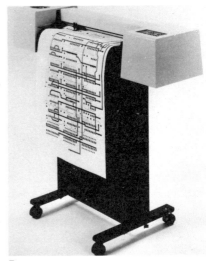

B

Questions

1   An architect is going to produce detailed plans for a new shopping centre. Suggest a suitable device on which the hard copy could be produced.
2   A small business uses computers for sending memos to members of staff, sending letters to customers, and printing a magazine which contains black and white text in a similar form to that in a newspaper. Given that the company has several microcomputers, what printers would you suggest are needed and why?

Storage Devices

Do you remember that computers have two main types of store? Can you remember what these were called?

Backing store (or secondary store) was the store used when the computer had to look after data that was not needed quickly and had to be stored for a considerable length of time.

Main store was the second type. This was the store used when the computer needed to access the data as quickly as possible. We will now look at some of the different types of backing store.

It is important to know why different types of backing store are more suitable for some applications than others. To be able to do this, we will now cover the main types of backing store used in modern computer systems.

Magnetic cassette tapes

These devices are similar to the audio cassettes that most people use at home. Indeed, such cassettes are often used as backing store on some microcomputer systems. A lot of software is also sold on cassette, especially home computer applications.

Magnetic tape has an advantage that it is very cheap. Unfortunately it is also very slow, and any data that happens to be at the wrong end of the tape can take a very long time indeed to find. If normal audio cassettes are used the system can also be unreliable. This can be overcome to some extent, but cassettes are not really satisfactory as backing store for serious home or business microcomputer users. Although several million characters may be stored on a cassette, the characters can only be read at about 120 per second which, in computer terms, is very slow indeed.

The data on tape is stored magnetically. You should therefore never place a magnet near to a tape or valuable data on the tape may be lost forever.

Large reel magnetic tape machines

On larger computers such as mainframes very different forms of magnetic tape are used. A typical magnetic tape unit for a mainframe is shown in Photograph A together with the tape.

These tape units are very expensive compared to domestic cassettes and often cost many thousands of pounds. However, they form a very reliable form of backing store and are especially useful when large amounts of data such as the processing of quarterly gas bills is required. Much data that is not needed immediately can be stored on tape. Indeed large tape libraries such as the one shown in Photograph B are often found in Government offices or very large businesses.

A

B

It is most important to realise that although tapes are ideal for processing vast amounts of data in a batch, they are not suitable for instantly finding a single item of information. When *batch processing* takes place, the data is usually arranged in alphabetical or some other convenient order so that each item of information can be processed one after the other. To gain access to a single item on a tape requires reading all the previous items until you get to the one you require. This method of accessing items of data one after the other is called *serial access*.

Several hundred million characters of information can be stored on a large reel of tape. It is also possible to read the data very quickly once you have found it. However, if a quick response to a query is required, then magnetic tape would not be suitable.

Questions

1 Why is cassette tape not very satisfactory as a backing storage device?
2 What is meant by the term serial access?
3 Give an example of the type of data that is ideal to be stored on large tape machines.

Magnetic Disks

There are several types of magnetic disks available. However, most of these different types of disks are used on micros. All are based on the idea that data is recorded onto a rotating magnetic surface. The disk spins around very quickly and it only takes a few fractions of a second for any item of data on the disk to be found. This can be compared with a maximum of a few minutes that could be necessary on a tape system.

The main difference between a tape and disk is that it is possible to access an item of data on disk without having to read all the items of data before it. This is known as *random access*. It is very fast compared with the serial access method when using tape. As with tape, the disks must be carefully looked after or data may be lost. The disks must be physically protected from heat and dust, and must never be brought anywhere near to a magnet. It is important to realise, especially when using computers at home, that things like hi-fi loudspeakers have powerful magnets inside them. It has been known for a disk to become corrupted (or spoilt) by simply leaving it on top of a loudspeaker. If this happens, you will never be able to recover your programs that are stored on disk. Always keep a backup copy that is put in a different place to the original.

Question

Why are disks better than tape if an item of data is needed very quickly?

Floppy disks

These are small flexible magnetic disks that are mainly used on microcomputer systems. The amount of data that can be stored on a floppy disk is very small compared to the amount of data that can be stored on tape, but it can be accessed very quickly. A typical floppy disk is shown in Photograph A.

A

There are various methods to increase the amount of data that can be stored on floppy disks. It is now possible to store about one or two million characters of information on a single disk.

Hard disks

These types of magnetic disks are mainly found on mini and mainframe computer systems. These hard disks were around long before the floppies. Indeed, floppy disks were called floppies because they were not hard and could flop about! A disk pack (hard disk) is inserted into the machine shown in the foreground of Photograph B.

Each pack contains several disk surfaces that revolve at very high speeds inside the disk machine. Up to about 200 million characters of information are almost instantly available when one of these hard disk systems is used. This makes it possible for vast amounts of data to be found very quickly indeed. An application where large amounts of data need to be accessed very quickly can be found in Airline Reservation booking systems. Most of the hard disk machines have to be operated in a clean air-conditioned room. This is usually the room in which the mainframe computer is also kept. Data can be accessed on hard disk several hundred times faster than on a floppy disk.

B

Winchester disks

This type of magnetic disk is also a hard disk, but the unit is much smaller than its big brother mentioned above. Also, the disk is entirely sealed and therefore no air-conditioned room is necessary. A typical Winchester disc unit is shown in Photograph C. They are ideal for use with the more expensive microcomputer systems, giving virtually instant access to up to about 30 million characters of information.

C

Task

Suggest a typical backing storage device for the following applications:
a) A home computer costing £100 used to play games.
b) A small home computer used for word processing.
c) A small business microcomputer.
d) Storing data that contains 1 000 000 addresses in alphabetical order. They do not have to be accessed quickly.
e) A kidney donor data bank.

The Computer's Main Store

We have seen from page 8 that the programs and data that are currently being used are stored in the computer's main store. There are several types of main store but all have one thing in common: the data contained inside the main store can be found extremely quickly. Indeed, 'extremely quickly' is an understatement. It is possible to find an item of data in much less than a millionth of a second! As this fast time is almost immediate, main store is also known as *immediate access store*. This vast speed is one of the reasons why computers can work through their instructions very quickly indeed. The reason why these devices are so fast is that they are electronic. i.e. they have no moving parts like the tapes or disks.

The most common type of main memory is called RAM. This means *Random Access Memory*. We have seen that random access means that you can find an item of data without having to read all previous items of data that are stored. RAM chips are shown in Photograph A.

RAM has one big disadvantage. If the power to the computer fails, then all the data stored in RAM will be lost forever. This is not the case with disk and tape where the data is stored permanently. This is another reason why RAM is only used to temporarily store data.

There are other electronic chips called ROMs. ROM means *Read Only Memory*. They are very similar to RAM chips in that they are random access and very fast indeed. However, you can only read data from these chips. You can't put your own data into them as you can with RAM. This might seem a disadvantage, but it is often necessary to store programs that never change inside the computer. For example, when you switch your microcomputer on it seems to know what to do. This is because it is following a program that is permanently stored inside a ROM chip. The big advantage of ROM is that the data is not lost if the power to the computer fails.

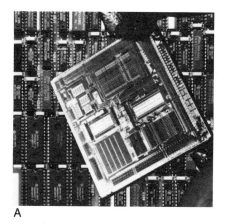

A

Questions

1 What is a hard disk? Would you ever fit one to your home computer? If so, which type?
2 What type of storage device would be ideal for a large travel agent who handles world wide booking of holidays?

3   What do the letters RAM and ROM stand for?
4   From which type of store can a computer get its data most
    quickly?
    Which type of store is the slowest?
5   What is the difference between backing (secondary) store and
    main store?
6   A school wishes to keep records of pupils on a computer
    system. If it is to be used by the office for enquiries such as:
    a) Is a pupil at school today?
    b) What form is Fred Billingsley in?
    c) Does Shiela Murray study geography etc.

    Suggest a suitable backing storage device for this system.
    Sometimes, a copy of all the data is made and kept in a safe
    place. This is in case of fire or damage to the system. On what
    form of storage do you suggest that these backups are made?

Software

We already know that computers need a set of instructions to
follow called a progam. Without this software, the computer
would not be able to do anything useful. We will now look in a
little more detail at these programs.

Types of software

Fortunately for many of us, people have written most of the
programs that we are ever likely to need. For example, you
may want a program to work out your business accounts, or
turn your computer into a word processor. Such programs can
be bought off the shelf from a computer store and are called
applications programs. There are literally thousands of
applications programs available for many different types of
computers. They are usually supplied on floppy disk together
with the user manuals which explain how to operate them.

There are also many ordinary but important tasks to be done
if you are to be able to get the best use from your computer
system. For example, it is necessary to be able to copy a disk,
load a program from a disk, or get the computer to output data
to a printer. All these things are often taken for granted, but
there are programs inside your computer, (often stored in
ROM) that enable you to do all of these things and many more.
These types of programs are written by the manufacturer of the
computer and are called *system software* i.e. software that
enables you to make use of the system easily.

Questions

1   Explain what is meant by software.
2   What is an applications program? Give some examples.
3   Why is system software usually supplied with each computer?

Solving a Problem

No matter how many applications programs are written there will always be some problems that you want to solve but no suitable programs are available. Also, many people actually enjoy writing programs and get a sense of achievement when they see even simple programs that they have written working on the computer.

Programs are really the final part of a lot of thought that has been put into solving a particular problem. The final result of a program can easily turn a computer into a word processor, a traffic light controller, a games player or a language teacher. Indeed whatever the programmer can dream up for the machine to do. Obviously the biggest problem is how do we go about solving the problem and eventually writing the program?

Describing the problem

Describing a problem in a way that makes it easy to solve on a computer means using a few techniques that have been developed for this purpose. But first let us concentrate on describing the problem.

In computing the set of 'rules' that (hopefully!) leads to the solution to a problem is called an *algorithm*. Although the word sounds quite complicated, the idea is very simple. The following is a set of instructions (algorithm) that enables a person to obtain a perfect piece of buttered toast.

Cut slice of bread to thickness required.
Place in toaster.
Switch on.
Keep looking until the toast is the right shade of brown.
When it is the right colour remove the bread.
If you like your toast hot, then butter it straight away,.
else leave it to cool and butter it later.
Eat it!

It is often easier to use pictures rather than words to communicate ideas. This is the idea behind one method called *flowcharts*.

Flowcharts

There are only four types of basic box and these are shown in Diagram A.

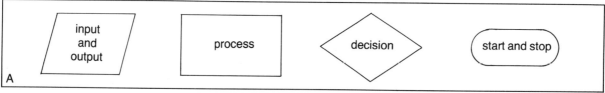

input and output   process   decision   start and stop

A

The use of each box is quite simple and can easily be guessed from its name. As an example of their use, consider the toast algorithm again. This time, a flowchart is used. The idea is shown in Diagram B. To understand the flowchart you should follow it through with your finger. The arrows indicate which way to go. You must do whatever is asked in the box before going onto the next box. When you come to the decision box, you must ask yourself the question and, based on the answer, follow the correct path away from the diamond shaped box.

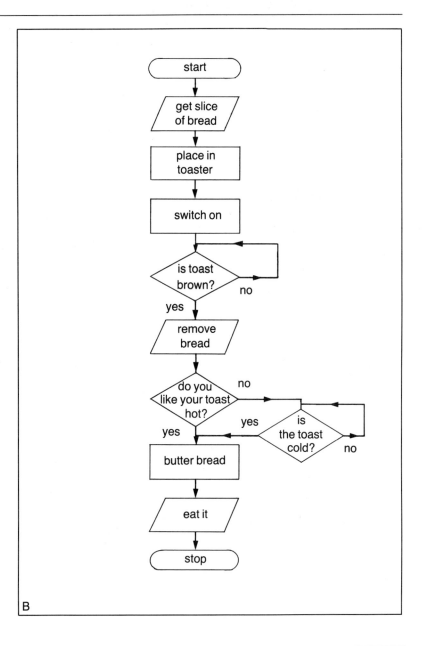

B

Task

1 Draw flowcharts which show how to do the following:
   a) Making a phone call. (You should allow for the line being engaged.)
   b) Running a computer program stored on a disk.

Questions

2 What is the name given to the set of instructions for the solution to a problem?
3 Draw a flowchart to solve the following:
   a) Making a cup of tea.
   b) Work out how much money you have at the end of the week.
   c) Sort out a list of five numbers into even or odd.
4 *Do* not write algorithms to solve the following problems. Just say if you think that they could be done. If not, why not?
   a) Converting text from German into English.
   b) Marking a mathematics test.
   c) Judging a beautiful baby competition.
   d) Working out the value of a famous painting.

Writing Your Own Programs

When you have designed a flowchart, the next stage is often writing the program. Now we already know that a program is a set of instructions that tell the computer what to do. But what instructions are available? This question depends upon many things and will now be looked at in more detail.

Programming languages

Programming computers used to be a very difficult and time consuming task. This was because all the instructions to the computer were written as patterns of 1's and 0's called *binary*. A typical pattern of digits that make up a program might have been:

> 01100111001001010111000101010101101010100
> 1100101101110101111101010101010101010100101
> 010101111000101100111101010000101011101
> 010100101001001001001111101001001001001

A single mistake in the above very simple program was difficult to find, and no help with finding errors was given by the computer. Developing programs in the above way was tedious, boring, time consuming and open to many errors.

Writing programs in the above way is called *machine code*. Even today, people have to write programs in machine code but a lot of help is available to them and nobody actually has to work out the patterns of binary numbers any more. Machine code is also called a *low level language* because it is a language that is able to communicate with the machine at an electronic level.

Machines are happy talking to each other in the above way, but it is more convenient for us to be able to use the language with which we are most familiar i.e. English. Unfortunately English is not a very precise language and even if it were possible for the computer to understand English, lots of mistakes would occur. For example, if you typed in the following sentence:

> I had a smashing experience yesterday.

Most people would realise that you had a good experience, but taken literally it could mean that you broke your best piece of china! English has too many double meanings for machines and so other, more precise languages have been developed. These new English-like languages are called *high level languages*. Languages such as English and French are high level because they are complicated and can be used to express many things. High level languages are also sometimes called *problem oriented languages* because they are often developed to help people solve specific types of problem. For example, COBOL is a language that helps people solve business problems.

Different types of high level languages

Most people who own a microcomputer will realise that there is a high level language called BASIC. This is a general purpose language that enables you to give instructions to your computer in a simple English-like way. For example, the following BASIC program prints out a name and address:

```
10  PRINT "Mr Arnie Ponsonby-Smythe"
20  PRINT "972, Sloane Square"
30  PRINT "London"
```

Notice that it is not the same as simply writing your address. For example, BASIC needs a line number at the beginning of every line. The computer needs to know that it must print the information it is given. The " marks tell the computer to print out the message between them. Finally, each line of the message in the program is printed on a new line when it is printed out.

There are many rules that you will have to learn if you write your own programs. The above are just some of the rules that BASIC requires.

A programming language is simply a convenient way of telling the computer exactly what you want it to do.

There are many different types of high level programming languages all designed for special purposes. For example, a mathematician needs to be able to cope with lots of complex formulae or a manager needs to be able to access large amounts of information quickly about the company's products. These two needs are very different and therefore different high level languages have been developed for each. FORTRAN is used by scientists and engineers, COBOL is used in large businesses, BASIC and PASCAL are used by students learning to program in schools and FORTH is used to help control robots. There are many of these *problem-oriented* languages all with their different rules and ways of doing this. However, they make life so much easier for the person who has to program the computer to do specific tasks.

Writing complex programs, even using a high level language is a difficult and time consuming task and requires a lot of thought and skill by the people involved. Often it takes years to develop some of the applications packages like accounting systems or word processors. If you do not need to write your own programs, then it is certainly easier, quicker and more cost effective to buy a ready-made package.

1 Make a list of as many high level programming languages that you can find. By the side of each language, write down what each language is mainly used for.

2 What is machine code?
3 Why is it easier to program in a high level language than a low level language?
4 Why is it necessary to have so many different types of high level languages?
5 Sometimes it is not a good idea to write your own programs, even though an application program might cost several hundred pounds. Why?
6 A friend of yours is convinced that, if you have a computer, then solving problems must be very easy. All you have to do is tell the computer what you want, and it gives you the answer! He has asked you to write him a 'little' program to work out his tax returns.

   Explain to your friend that his ideas of computers are not quite right. Also, give some examples of the sort of planning you would have to do, so that your friend will be convinced that it is *not* simply a matter of asking the computer for the answers.

Communications

One of the biggest growth areas in computing over the last few years has been in the field of *communications* i.e. getting computers to transmit information quickly and efficiently from one place to another. Most people have heard the expression 'we live in an information society': this has been brought about by the ability of computers to communicate with each other at very high speed. It is now cheaper and quicker to send a letter via a satellite than to send it by air mail. The aeroplane may take up to a day to arrive, the computer satellite link takes a few seconds!

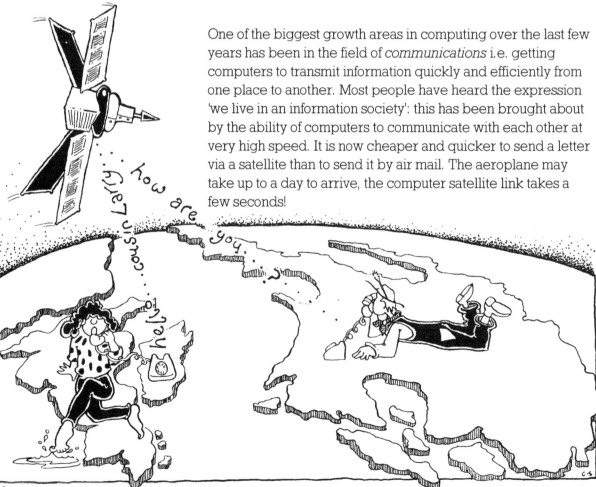

Connecting computers together

If two computers are close together then it is usually possible to have a cable that connects them so that information can be passed from one machine to another. However, this would not be convenient if they were 100 miles apart. Therefore, methods have been devised of connecting computers together by using the telephone system. The idea is shown in Diagram A.

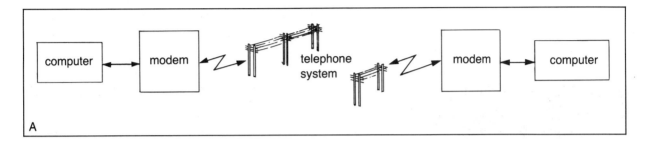

A

A special box called a *modem* is required so that signals from the computer can be converted into a form suitable to be sent over the telephone system. When the signals are received at the other end of the line, another modem is required to convert the signals back again. Each modem plugs into a special socket which is connected to the telephone system. A typical modem is shown in Photograph B.

An alternative method of connecting the computer is to make use of an *acoustic coupler*. This is not as satisfactory as the modem but with this method you don't need a special telephone socket. The handset of a normal telephone is placed in the acoustic coupler as shown in Photograph C. This is particularly useful if you are sending information back to the office from a portable computer.

Questions

1 Why do computers need to communicate with each other?
2 What is a modem?
3 What is an acoustic coupler?
4 Why are modems and acoustic couplers needed?

B

C

Prestel

The reason you need to connect computers together is usually because information is required that is not stored on your local computer. For example, suppose that you have a microcomputer and a telephone at home. If you are lucky you may have a floppy disk drive on which to store programs and data. It would not be sensible for you to store information about the flight times of all the airlines, the latest share prices on the Stock Exchange or the latest news or sports headlines. First you would not have the storage space on your disk (even if you had hundreds of them!), and secondly, it would not be possible for you to keep the information up to date even if you could find all the information.

British Telecom realised some years ago that there was a need for such information. They set up several mainframe computers around the country with an extremely large amount of information stored on them. Anyone with a phone, modem and a computer (or indeed a special unit that could be plugged into a TV) could access information from their system which is called *Prestel*. A typical page of information from Prestel is shown in Photograph A.

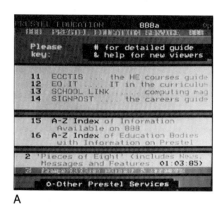

A

You can appreciate that such a vast undertaking would need a lot of business and other organisations to contribute to it. For example, the flight times of British Airways planes would have to be provided by British Airways, or the latest bargain holidays would be provided by different travel agents etc. All the businesses that contribute to the information stored on Prestel and similar systems are called *information providers*, or simply IPs.

It is very easy for you to save the page of information that is displayed on your computer screen onto your local discs. This means that you can browse through the information that you have chosen to save at a later time without the need to contact the Prestel computer.

Sometimes the IPs provide their information free of charge. Often however, you will find that you have to pay for the information before you can look at it. This charge is in addition to the telephone bill and the charge made by British Telecom for belonging to Prestel. The reason why some companies make a charge is that the information they provide is very specialised, or can be used by other businesses to make money.

Each IP has to pay British Telecom for the privilege of storing information on their system. Even if the IPs do not charge for the information they provide, they can often get their money back from the increased business that is generated by the people looking at their company on the Prestel system.

1 What is Prestel and who runs it?
2 What hardware is needed to connect a computer to the Prestel system?
3 Can you use the Prestel system if you don't have a home computer?
4 What costs are involved in using the Prestel system?
5 Who are the Information Providers and what do they do?
6 Why do IPs sometimes charge for the information they provide?

Orders by computer

In addition to browsing through the information some IPs provide the facility to order goods. For example, if you were browsing through some of the wine suppliers you may see a case of your favourite vintage that takes your fancy. You can then go through a simple procedure which allows you to place an order for the wine. The supplier knows who you are and where to send the goods because of your unique Prestel customer number. The name and address can be got from the Prestel computer and the goods dispatched the same day. You can often quote a credit card number so that the bill can be paid by this method if you prefer. Anything from wine and spirits to theatre tickets can be booked via the Prestel computer. However, sometimes, booking things like airline tickets is restricted to business users such as travel agents etc. Also, there are private pages of information which only certain people with the appropriate pass codes can see.

Electronic mail

Prestel is a two-way communication link. This means that you can send messages to Prestel as well as receive information from them. Also, there is a system called an *electronic mailbox* which means that you can send and receive letters from your friends and business colleagues who are also members of the Prestel system. The ideas are simple and are shown in Diagram B.

Diagram B shows Karen contacting the Prestel computer and writing a letter which is stored in the electronic mailbox on the Prestel computer. At some time later, her friend David contacts the Prestel computer and asks the computer to see if their is any mail for him. The computer then gives David access to the letters that belong to him. After reading through the mail on his own computer David sees Karen's letter and replies to it by typing on his own computer, and sending a copy to Prestel's electronic mailbox ready for Karen to see the next time she contacts the Prestel computer. See Diagram C.

Prestel computer centre

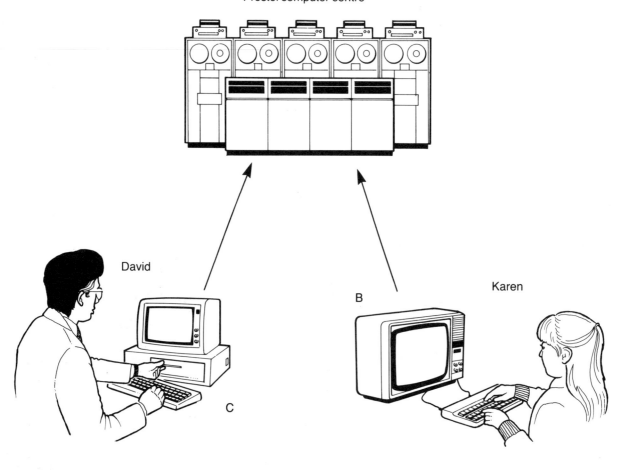

David

B

Karen

C

Questions

1 Make a list of three companies that allow you to order goods or services over the Prestel system.
2 What is an electronic mailbox?
3 Can you look at all the pages of information on the Prestel system? If not, why not?

Security on the System

Disastrous consequences could arise if anyone broke into the system illegally. You can imagine 100 boxes of writing paper arriving on your doorstep when you did not order them! A system of *passwords* and *customer numbers* is used to make the system as secure as possible.

Teletext services

One of the disadvantages with the Prestel system is that it is expensive for the ordinary person. You have to pay telephone bills, charges to British Telecom, charges to the IPs and buy some expensive equipment such as computers and modems. A much cheaper alternative (but far less versatile) is the *teletext service* provided by the BBC and IBA Television companies. The BBC's teletext service is called *Ceefax* and the IBA's teletext service is called *Oracle*.

Anyone with a specially equipped TV set can receive the codes that are sent with the normal TV pictures. Information, much the same as some of that found on Prestel can then be displayed on your TV screen. The system is very useful as you can easily browse through the latest news and sports headlines, look at what the weather is going to do, or find out some of the latest holiday bargains. However, the big disadvantage is that the system is not two-way. This means that you can't send messages back to the system to order crates of wine or holidays as you could with the Prestel service.

The above disadvantage is not as drastic as it sounds because you can easily pick up the telephone and order your holiday from the travel agent who was advertising on the Teletext service. However, by the time you get through they may have all gone! Another disadvantage with teletext services is that they are only transmitted when the TV stations are on the air. This means that you could not find out any information at all at three in the morning, but the teletext system is good, very useful and free!

Both the Prestel and teletext systems are examples of what are called *viewdata systems*.

Questions

1 Who runs the teletext services?
2 Can an ordinary TV display the teletext signals?
3 What are the advantages of teletext over Prestel?
4 List three advantages of Prestel over teletext.

Networks

In addition to the viewdata services mentioned above, computers are often connected together in other ways. If you have a computer at home you will appreciate that buying a disk drive and printer often costs more than the original computer.

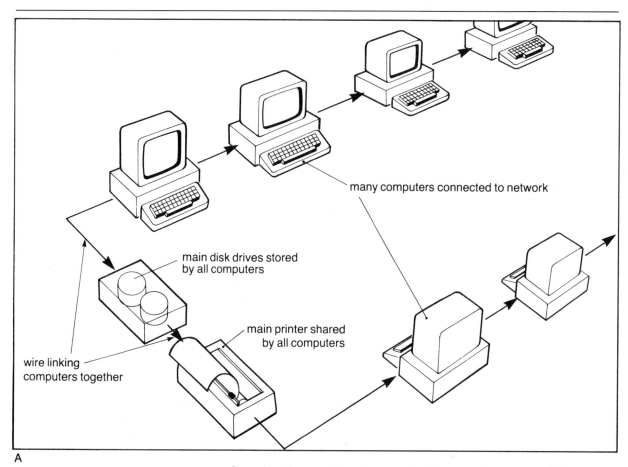

A

Imagine the problem in school where a classroom of 26 computers are needed. You would need 26 extra disk drives and 26 extra printers if everybody is going to be happy.

One alternative is to have fewer disk drives and printers and to move them around the room to where they are needed, but this is very slow and is likely to damage the equipment after a while. A better alternative is to devise a system where all the computers can share a single disk drive and printer. Such a system is shown in Diagram A and is called a *network*.

It is usual to have a better type of disk drive than you would normally have had on a single computer and so Winchester disk drives are often chosen for their greater speed and greater storage capacities than floppies. Although the Winchester is more expensive, and some complex software is needed to organise the network, the overall system is very much cheaper than everybody having their own disk drive and printer.

Networks need not be restricted to a single classroom. Indeed many schools now have computer networks extending throughout a building or the whole school site. Businesses are often linked together via local area networks and if the computers are a long distance apart then the telephone system can also be used.

There are several large nationwide networks and some networks are actually worldwide. However, the principles are similar to the classroom example given at the beginning of this section.

1 Why are computers sometimes connected together as a network?
2 A travel agent has access to both Prestel and teletext. However, he finds that, even though the holidays are advertised on teletext, the Prestel system is much more useful. Why do you think that this is so? Do you think that it would be a good idea for travel agents to set up a national network of computers. If so, why?

If you have a network in your school or college, find out the following information:
3 Who is in charge of the network?
4 How many computers are connected to it?
5 What type of disk does the network have?
6 Are there any printers connected to the network? If so, how many?
7 How do you become a user of the network?

Computer Files

In any large office there is usually a filing cabinet containing many folders in which *files* of information are stored. The number of files and information in these files will depend on the business, but we will consider a simple example:

In the 'Oriental' grocer's shop there are several files of information. Some of these files together with examples are given in the following list:

(File 1) Customers' name and address file (including telephone number and amount outstanding).

Example of file entry...

Name	Gladys Emanuel
Address	23 Station Road, Bolton
Telephone number	(0772) 385467
Amount outstanding	£14.70 (i.e. Credit)

(File 2) Supplier's file

Example of file entry...

Name	Yummy Yummy Biscuits Ltd.
Address	126 High Street, Reading, Berkshire
Telephone Number	(0528) 32371

(File 3) Stock list file

Example of file entry...

		Number in stock	Number on order
Supplier	Yummy Yummy Biscuits		
Item 1	Digestives...	27 packets	150 packets
Item 2	All Butter Munch...	24 packets	200 packets

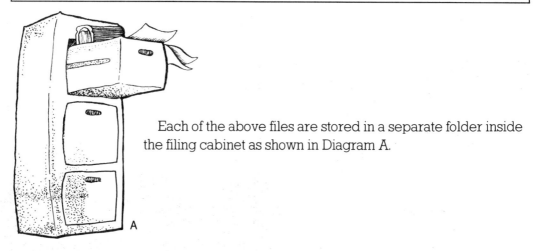

Each of the above files are stored in a separate folder inside the filing cabinet as shown in Diagram A.

Question

Write down some more information that could be stored in
a) Customers' name and address file.
b) Supplier's file.
c) Stock list file.

Problems to be solved

Mr Rahanji Singh, the grocer, is fed up with time spent during the evening working out what items to order and what bills etc. need paying. After many years of living with a cash register that does not work he has finally decided to find out how a microcomputer could be used to help him with his problems. Unfortunately, Mr Singh does not understand any of the computer jargon and so Chris, the shop assistant, who has been on a computer awareness course, decides to explain it to him. This is done in the next section.

Question

Describe the operations that would have to be carried out when obtaining information from a file which is stored in a filing cabinet.

Files on Computer

Most of the computer terms associated with files are taken from the normal words that are used everyday in the office. The computer term *file* has exactly the same meaning as the office file described above. A file is simply a collection of records that are related in some way to each other. For example, the customer names and addresses file mentioned above. Each file entry is called a *record*. Therefore, Gladys Emanuel's entry containing her name, address, telephone number and amount outstanding is referred to as Gladys Emanuel's record in the customer name and addresses file.

Fields

There are four fields in Gladys Emanuel's record. These are the 'name', 'address', 'telephone number' and the 'amount outstanding'fields. The idea is shown in Diagram B.

B	Name	Gladys Emanuel
	Address	23 Station Road, Bolton
	Telephone number	(0772) 385467
	Amount outstanding	£14.70 (i.e. Credit)

Question

How many fields are there in
a) the supplier's file record?
b) in the stock list file record?

Key field

It is usual to give each record a specific name. This is usually the most important field or the field containing the information by which the record is know. In computing this is called the *key field*, or simply *key*. In our example, using the customer name and address file, the key field would be customer name. This is the information that is used to find a record in the file.

Question

What are the names given to the key field in
a) the supplier's record file?
b) the stock list file?

Characters

In computing it is necessary to split up the field into a more basic unit called a character. A character is simply a letter or a number etc. If we look at the amount outstanding field of Gladys Emanuel's record and count up the characters, we can see that it contains six characters. i.e.

Amount outstanding field	£	1	4	.	7	0
Character numbers	1	2	3	4	5	6

It is important to realise that a space or other special symbols are also counted as characters. Therefore the following field has 22 characters:

23 Station Road Bolton

Question

How many characters are there in the supplier's file, telephone number field?

How many characters in the field?

It is important to know how many characters will be in a particular field because the number of characters is usually limited. For example, suppose that only fifteen characters were available to enter a name. i.e.

Name _ _ _ _ _ _ _ _ _ _ _ _ _ _ _

If you happened to be called Jeremiah Ponsonby-Smythe, then your name would have to be shortened, perhaps to something like:

Name J _ Pon _ Smythe _ _ _

Question

Choose some suitable names if the following people had to be stored using only fifteen characters.
a) Christopher Wynniatt-Hussey
b) James Bond
c) Veronica Warburton
d) Winston Robinson

How much space?

It is important when designing records on a computer that a sensible amount of space is used for each field. Too little and you get many of the problems shown above. Too much, and a lot of space is wasted on the computer. Similarly, it would be sensible to stick to one method such as initials and surname, or allow just a little more space if first names are to be included.

Questions

1   In computer terms, what is meant by a file?
2   By using a suitable example, explain how characters, fields and records make up a file.
3   What is meant by a key field?
4   Suggest a suitable key field, and other fields that might be found in records contained in the following files:
    a) An airline reservation system
    b) A bank account
    c) The police criminal records system
    d) A library

Special Techniques

A

When a computer system is used, instead of being stored on pieces of card or paper in a filing cabinet, the files are stored on media such as tape or disk. (Media is just the general name for the materials on which the information is stored.) It is not necessary to understand the detail of how this information is stored because the programs inside the computer make it easy for the person using the computer to enter or take out the information, as though they were dealing with a filing cabinet, files and pieces of paper. Some systems use *icons*. These are little pictures on the screen similar to that shown Photograph A.

Some systems are so *user friendly* (easy to use) that pictures of a filing cabinet with its drawer open will appear on the screen when you open a file. The system will ask you to enter the key field and then the appropriate record will be found and displayed on the screen. Compare this with going to the filing cabinet, opening the drawer, taking out the correct file, opening the file and thumbing through until you find the right record, then placing the piece of paper in front of you on the desk. The only difference with the computer is that the record is now displayed on the screen and has been found in a fraction of the time taken to do it manually. Most of the modern systems are *mouse driven* (as shown in Photograph A), and the majority of them include a picture of a *dustbin*. Move the cursor on the screen over the dustbin, press the button on the mouse and you have just thrown the information on the screen into the dustbin! i.e. got rid of it. This is very handy if you make a complete mess of filling in the information. You simply start again as though you had a fresh piece of paper.

Task

1 Get your teacher to demonstrate how it is possible to access some information from a computer. Write down the name of the file used, and suitable names for the records in the file. Write down three examples of information that can be obtained from the system.

Questions

2 What is meant by user friendly?
3 What is meant by the word media?
4 On what media could the following be stored?
   a) Information in a filing cabinet
   b) A computer file.

File Processing

Computers are often processing a lot of data contained in files. Indeed it has been estimated that over 80% of the computing power today is used just for this purpose. This is quite an eye opener for the people who think that most computers spend their time doing long and complicated maths calculations. As most computers are used to process files this is an important section to understand.

You should now have a good idea about what a file is, and how the data contained in the file is organised. We will now concentrate on how these files are used in *data processing*.

The large computer system

Most of the work in this section will be related to what is done on larger computers rather than on the home micros. You are advised to look back at Photograph C on page 11 which shows a mainframe computer with a number of hard disk machines. This will be the equipment that will mainly be used throughout this section. However, the principles can and are applied to much smaller computer systems.

Typical processes in data processing

Many thousands of files can be kept on magnetic disks. These files contain much information. Typical examples would be criminal records or rates demands. The information contained in these files may be different, but the processes carried out by the computers are similar.

Question

Why is file processing a very important part of computing?

44

Basic File Operations

Information contained in files often becomes out of date, i.e. a customer may have changed their address or some money owing to a business may have been paid. This means that it is necessary to update the information contained in the files. This process is called *updating*.

Before a record can be *updated* it must be found. Also, if the information is to be displayed on a VDU screen then the file and record must also be found. The process of looking for a record within a file is called *searching*.

Sometimes, the data contained in the file might need sorting into a different order. Often different departments within a business require the information to be presented in different ways. If the data has to be rearranged into a different order, then this process is called *sorting*.

Updating, searching and sorting are major operations that go on when files are being processed.

There is another operation that is used when processing files and this is called *merging*. Merging is quite simple and is particularly suited to tape machines. Consider the tape file shown in Diagram A.

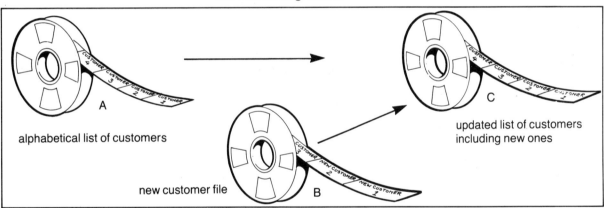

alphabetical list of customers

new customer file

updated list of customers including new ones

Diagram A shows part of the customer records file in a department store. Let us suppose that during the week two new customers apply for and are given permission to open accounts at the store. Diagram B shows the file of new customers for the week. At the end of the week it is decided to update the master file. This is done by merging the new customer file with the old master file to produce a new master file. This process is shown in Diagram C. Similar processes can also be done on magnetic disk but more sophisticated methods are usually used if the files are stored on disks. See also payrolls on page 65.

Explain what is meant by the following processes:
a) Updating,
b) Searching,
c) Sorting,
d) Merging.

Sorting Example

You may have information in a file in a form that is not suitable for other purposes. For example, look at the following records from a file where name is chosen as the key field:

Name	Form	Subjects Studied and Exam Result
Bortoft	4d	Maths 47, Physics 89, Ballet Dancing 03
Bradley	4a	Maths 87, Physics 91, Computing 100
Camellini	4b	Chemistry 78, Biology 26, Physics 58
Cummings	4e	Geography 85 Computing 67, Woodwork 59
Dennis	4f	Biology 76, Art 38, English 69
Fothergill	4a	Maths 47, Computing 95, Biology 86

In this file records are stored in alphabetical student name. This is ideal when an enquiry of the sort 'What grade did Bortoft get for maths?' is made. However, if the head of computing wanted a list of all the computing grades in rank order (i.e. who came top, who came next etc.) then the computer would have to go through a two stage process.

1 The computer would have to go through the file and extract all the records of the students who take computing. In the above simple case this would be:

Bradley	4a	Maths 87, Physics 91, Computing 100
Cummings	4e	Geography 85, Computing 67, Woodwork 59
Fothergill	4a	Maths 47, Computing 95, Biology 86

2 The computer would then have to *sort* the file into rank order of computing results. Also, in this case, other subject data would not be required. Therefore the output from this sorting process could be.

Details of computer studies results 1987

Name	Form	%
Bradley	4a	100
Fothergill	4a	95
Cummings	4e	67

Obviously in a real example there would be much more detail. However, the principles of sorting would be the same.

Questions

1 Using the example given in this section, make a list of the physics grades together with student names in order, highest first.
2 Using the example given in this section, make a list of the biology grades together with student names in order, highest first.

3   A microcomputer dealer thinks that a computer system may
    help run the sales side of the business. On this computer, they
    expect to be able to store information such as:

    Manufacturer, type, RAM size etc.

    a) When setting up the files on the computer, what do you think
       would be useful information to use as the *key field* and why?
    b) Write down ten different pieces of information that you think
       ought to be included about each computer sold.
    c) The new computer system will be used to perform the
       following operations:

    Search, update and sort

    Give a typical example of what would happen when each of
    the above operations are carried out on the system.

More Flowchart Symbols

It is far easier to draw diagrams showing file operations than to
talk about them. Some extra flowchart symbols have been
developed for this purpose. They are shown in Diagram A.
These flowcharts are called *systems flowcharts* because they
show how the computer system is to be used to solve a
problem.

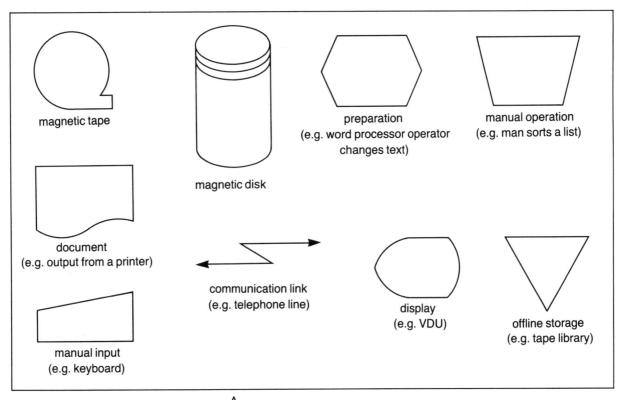

A

Systems flowcharts are quite simple and the easiest way to
understand them is to use them. As an example, we will
develop a systems flowchart to show the operations carried out

in the sort example given in the last section. Diagram B shows a possible system flowchart for the problem of extracting the computing grades from the students files.

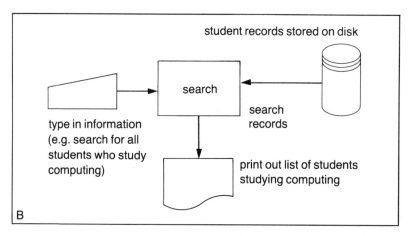

student records stored on disk

search

type in information (e.g. search for all students who study computing)

search records

print out list of students studying computing

B

Keeping backup copies of important files

It is essential that backup copies are made of all files. If this is not done, and a file is damaged, then the data will be lost forever.

Information can be lost through human carelessness, incorrect data being typed in which deletes the older correct data, through a hardware fault in the computer disk or tape (much less likely), or through disasters like the computer room being burnt down (even less likely). However, if the data is very important then all these possibilities have to be allowed for.

Damage to the disk by fire can only be catered for by having a copy of the original tape or disk in a different building. This is actually done and large tape and disk libraries are often set up using fire proof boxes stored in other buildings.

Damage to the disk by a hardware fault can be overcome by keeping copies of the disk and tapes separate from the originals. But what about damage by typing in the wrong data? We could keep a copy of all the old files, but this would get ridiculous after a few years as there would be no space to store them. Also, it is likely that the original data may not be of much use after a certain amount of time. e.g. do you really need to know how much your electricity bill was five years ago?

We have to make a compromise between being able to recover original information and not having too many files around which contain very similar information. This is shown in the next section.

Questions

1 Why are systems flowcharts useful?
2 What is meant by a backup copy?
3 Why is it important to make backups? Give three different reasons.

Grandfather Father Son Principle

This is a method that has been developed to keep a number of backup copies. The terms *master file* and *transaction file* now need to be understood. A simple example will help.

Suppose that we run a credit card company. We will probably have a large file which contains all the information about customers' names and addresses, amount outstanding etc. This file would be an example of a master file.

Now during any month, there will be a large number of transactions (purchases etc.) made by many of the customers. As the monthly returns come in from the shops all over the country a transaction file is gradually built up for the current month. At the end of the month, the transaction file would be sorted into an order which matches the master file. For example, both the master and transaction files could be sorted on credit card number.

The next stage of the process would be to update the old master file by merging it with the transaction file. This process is shown in Diagram A.

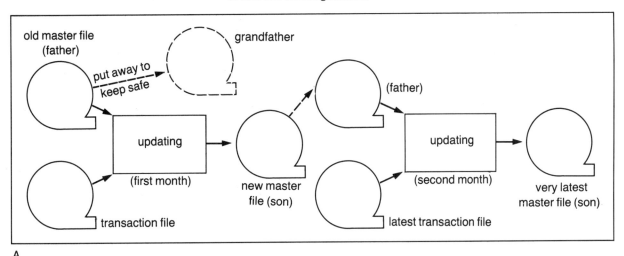

A

During the merge, the old master file records are updated if necessary and each record in the old master file is copied onto the new master file together with any update that was contained in the transaction file.

At the end of the first month we have produced a new master file which is called the *son*. The old master file is now called the *father*. Both father and son files together with the transaction file are put away for safe-keeping.

During the next month a new transaction file will be built up from the transactions that have taken place during the next month. At the end of the second month, the latest transaction file is used to update the latest master file as shown in the second half Diagram A. The *very latest master file* is now called the *son*, the *master file* that was used to produce it is called the *father*, and the *oldest master file* is now called the *grandfather*.

In the above way, *three generations of files* are kept safe. Any mistake that was entered in either of the two months can be recovered because we have all the old information. It is found in practice that it is not usually necessary to keep the very old files when the next months transactions take place and so, after the third month, the original master file would no longer be needed. The disk or tape which contained the old master file can then be used again for other purposes.

1 What is a master file? What is a transaction file? Give examples.
2 Most of the file operations described in this section could be done without computers. Why are computers used?
3 Explain the terms grandfather, father and son files.

Batch and Real Time

In the above example we saw how the transaction file was used to update the master file once a month. Such a job would usually take place on a mainframe computer overnight and the bills be sent to the customers within a few days. It may take several days or weeks before a transaction that takes place in a shop actually gets transferred into the computer system. All the work submitted to the computer is done in a *batch*. This is a very efficient way of getting an expensive computer system to process vast amounts of information very quickly. Such a system is called *batch processing*.

Consider now the problem of booking an airline ticket. It would be most inconvenient if the travel agent said 'come back next week and I will tell you if there is one available'! You might want to get on the plane that afternoon. Such an enquiry must be dealt with immediately by the computer system. This is not just so the customer knows straight away, but so that no other customer anywhere in the world can book the same ticket for the same seat in the same plane. A system which can give you a response almost immediately is said to be working in *real time*. A computer which is able to work like this is said to be doing *real time processing*.

Most mainframes are so powerful that they can do both real time and batch processing at the same time!

1 Batch processing and real time processing are ideal for certain jobs. Explain each term and give an example where each type of system could be used.
2 State whether batch processing or real time processing would be suitable for the following applications:
   a) A car hire firm which uses a computer to confirm bookings.
   b) A supermarket to send out bills to customers.
   c) A police criminal records computer.
   d) A monthly book club.

Programming

It is not important on a computer awareness course to be able to write complex programs of your own. Indeed it would take a book much longer than this one just to teach you how to write even simple programs.

It is likely that your teacher will get you to write a few simple programs to give you an idea of what it involves, but the important thing is to realise why and how programs are written and what processes are involved when other people write them for you. There is nothing worse than asking someone to write a program for you and not understanding some of the problems that they will have to overcome. All too often people ask for ridiculous things or do not realise the tremendous amount of work that is necessary to produce good software.

Often the author has been asked by an innocent friend 'Can you please just write me a program to do this or that', when you say that you have just asked me to undertake about six months work, the people are astounded, apologise and say they did not realise it was that involved!

Defining your problem

We have already seen that it is important for the problem to be solved to be well defined. If this is not done then it is likely that the end result will not be what the user wanted.

Program structure

After the problem has been properly worked out it is the task of the programmer to code the problem using a suitable high level language. Over the last few years much argument has gone on about which languages are better than others. However, the biggest problem is can people understand your program? If they can't, then it is not very useful.

The above may sound a little strange. Why is a program not useful if it works? The answer to this question depends on what the program does. Consider the following:

1   If you are writing a program for yourself, then as long as it works, it may be very useful to you. It may even be very useful to somebody else if it does exactly what they want.

2   In industry, programs written professionally are often used by many different companies. It is likely that these programs will have to be modified as the needs of the business change. (They always do!)

It may be that after two or three years some modifications to the programs are necessary. It is also highly likely that the people who have to modify these programs are not the same people as those who wrote them.

It is essential that the original programs are well written and easy to understand by the new people. If not, much time will have been wasted. In industry time means money. If a job takes more time than is absolutely necessary, then the cost of even a simple modification could be very high indeed.

Many rules have been worked out by experienced people that make programs much easier to understand. Indeed, some new high level computer languages have even been developed for this very purpose. The main techniques that are used are called *structured programming*.

What is structure in a program?

Structure simply means a well defined plan. One structured way of planning a program is to split up the task to be undertaken into sub-tasks. An example is shown in Diagram A.

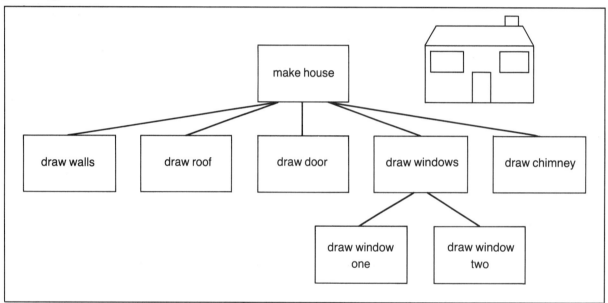

A

The task of drawing a house on the screen has been planned. It has been split up into five sub-tasks. Draw main block, draw roof, put in door, put in windows and draw chimney.

The plan has been devised so that different people could do the different sub-tasks. This is exactly how professional programs are written in industry.

Designing the plan is *not* the same as writing the program. The program to draw the house on the screen of a BBC micro is shown in Diagram B.

Diagram C shows a program to perform the same task. It is written in an unstructed way. There are no well defined sub-tasks, and it is not easy to follow.

The above techniques can be easily applied to very much more complex programs. For example, if each sub-task is complicated, all that is needed is to split up the complex sub-task into even smaller modules. In this way teams of people can be used to write very complex software.

Although you may have done it several times it is not very efficient to sit down at the keyboard without some well thought out plan in your mind and, preferably, on a piece of paper. This

```
 10 PROCdraw_walls
 20 PROCdraw_roof
 30 PROCdraw_door
 40 PROCdraw_windows
 50 PROCdraw_chimney
 60 END
100 DEFPROCdraw_
    walls
110    MOVE 200,200
120    DRAW 200,500
130    DRAW 700,500
140    DRAW 700,200
150    DRAW 200,200
160 ENDPROC
200 DEFPROCdraw_
    roof
210    MOVE 200,500
220    DRAW 300,650
230    DRAW 600,650
240    DRAW 700,500
250 ENDPROC
300 DEFPROCdraw_
    door
310    MOVE 400,200
320    DRAW 400,400
330    DRAW 500,400
340    DRAW 500,200
350 ENDPROC
400 DEFPROCdraw_
    windows
410    REM window one
420    MOVE 250,350
425    DRAW 250,450
430    DRAW 350,450
435    DRAW 350,350
440    DRAW 250,350
445    REM window two
450    MOVE 550,350
455    DRAW 550,450
460    DRAW 650,450
465    DRAW 650,350
470    DRAW 550,350
480 ENDPROC
500 DEFPROCdraw_
    chimney
510    MOVE 500,650
520    DRAW 500,725
530    DRAW 575,725
540    DRAW 575,650
550 ENDPROC
```

B

```
110    MOVE 200,200
120    DRAW 200,500
130    DRAW 700,500
140    DRAW 700,200
150    DRAW 200,200
210    MOVE 200,500
220    DRAW 300,650
230    DRAW 600,650
240    DRAW 700,500
310    MOVE 400,200
320    DRAW 400,400
330    DRAW 500,400
340    DRAW 500,200
420    MOVE 250,350
430    DRAW 350,450
440    DRAW 250,350
450    MOVE 550,350
455    DRAW 550,450
460    DRAW 650,450
465    DRAW 650,350
470    DRAW 550,350
510    MOVE 500,650
520    DRAW 500,725
530    DRAW 575,725
540    DRAW 575,650
```

C

may not seem important to you when you are writing simple programs, but it is essential when writing long and complex programs.

It is most important to appreciate that the costs of developing professionally written software are extremely high. In fact, the software costs for microcomputer systems often exceed the cost of the hardware. It is for this reason that professional software writers approach their task with well written algorithms. Each stage is planned in great detail before the programs are written. It is essential to get the program right the first time round, otherwise it could be very expensive to modify at some later stage.

To give you an idea of the costs of writing software, a very well written game for a microcomputer may cost about five thousand pounds to develop. At the other end of the scale, software for a large banking mainframe computer could cost several million pounds.

Questions

1 Why is it necessary to plan a program carefully before writing the code?
2 Why is it important to write your programs so that they can be understood by other people?
3 Why is software usually expensive?

Program Structures

Most high level languages provide basic structures which enable programs to be written in easily understood terms. The most common structures are *loops* and *branches*. These will now be looked at in more detail.

Loops

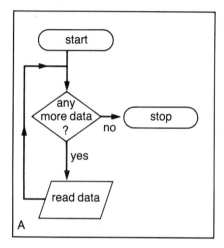

In computing, processes often have to be repeated over and over again. For example, data may have to be read in from a file until there is no more data left. This forms a natural loop and is shown in Diagram A.

One method of coding the above loop in some high level language is by using the REPEAT UNTIL structure. This is as follows:

```
REPEAT
   READ data from file
UNTIL no more data is left
```

Branches

One of the most powerful abilities of a computer is to be able to make decisions based on the results of a test. For example, is a number too big or too small, is a temperature too high or too low? etc. To be able to make decisions like this involves the use of a structure known as a *branch*. We have seen the use of a branch before when flowcharts were covered.

A typical branch structure is an IF THEN structure. For example, suppose that we were monitoring the temperature of a central heating system. In a typical high level language this might be coded as follows:

```
READ temperature
IF temperature is greater than 21°C
THEN switch off heater.
```

Many of these branch structures can make a computer appear to have intelligence. This is because it appears that the computer 'knows' what to do in every situation that is likely to occur. However, if a situation occurs for which the computer has not been properly programmed to cope, then the correct decision will not be made.

Questions

1 How is a complicated task split up so that many different people can help in writing the same program?
2 What is meant by the following terms:
   a) Branch,
   b) Loop?

Computers in the Home

The last few years have seen a big increase in the number of microcomputers used in the home. Many people use computers at home for entertainment, linking up to banking systems, or keeping information about their businesses. A typical microcomputer system is shown in Photograph A.

A

Inside the microcomputer is a powerful electronic chip called a *microprocessor*. This is the part of the system that is used to control all the operations that go on inside the machine.

As well as the microcomputers themselves, many people have computers inside their homes without realising it. Such computers can be found inside washing machines, teletext television sets and microwave cookers. In fact these computers are very small and are built around the microprocessor. They are *not* the same as microcomputers, because they obviously have no keyboards, VDU's or disk drives etc.

As an example, consider the electronic washing machine shown in Diagram B

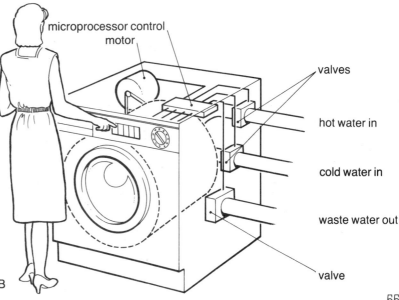

B

The microprocessor inside the machine receives its instructions from the buttons pushed by the person operating the machine. When the correct set of buttons have been pushed, the microprocessor control unit controls all the operations needed to do the washing. For example, the following programme might be used for washing coloured clothes:

1 Fill tub with warm water.
2 Agitate tub for 5 minutes.
3 Drain water.
4 Rinse with cold water.
5 Spin.
6 Stop.

Microprocessors are used inside many devices because they are *fast, small, reliable* and *cheap.*

Task

1 A system has been installed inside a house to make it look like someone is at home when they are in fact out. It does this by switching the lights on and off in every room during the evening. If this anti-burglar device is controlled by a microprocessor, write down a suitable set of instructions that could be used to develop a program to make the burglars think that someone is home between 6 p.m. and midnight.

Questions

2 Why is a microprocessor not a microcomputer?
3 List three reasons why microprocessors are used to control devices such as microwave ovens and washing machines.
4 Find out and list five different microprocessor controlled devices used in the home.
5 A small microprocessor-controlled robot is advertised as being the ideal home help. This is obviously not true. Why do you think this is so, and what are some of the things which limit the robot's ability to be able to do any job in the home?

*Services to the Community*____

Computers serve the community in many ways. In fact, without computers, some of the things which are done today would be almost impossible. Some typical examples are as follows.

Banking

Computers are used for many purposes by banks. We have already seen on page 14 how the clearing bank system relies on MICR characters. Another obvious application of interest to customers is the cash point machines that have now become such a common sight in most high streets. Many of these systems are linked up nationally by computers. The cash point terminal is linked to a computer so that it can give customers information about the current balance in their account, request statements, or check to see that sufficient funds are available before dispensing the cash.

The information provided by these cash point machines is obviously confidential, and the security of the system is a two-stage process. First you need to have a plastic card with a magnetic strip on it. Secondly, after putting the card into the machine, you have to type in a pass code. Without the card, people typing in codes can't enter the system. Without the pass code, people who steal the card can't use it. It is essential that you never write down your pass code and leave it together with your cash point card.

Task

1 Find out three different facilities that are available when using cash points at building societies.

Questions

2 Why would it be difficult for a thief who has stolen a cash point card to get money from a machine?
3 Name two uses of computers in banks besides cash points and clearing cheques.

Point of sale terminals

At the checkout of a modern supermarket you will probably find what is called a *point of sale terminal* (POS). One of these is shown in Photograph A (overleaf).

POS terminals provide a great variety of facilities for both the customer and the supermarket. POS terminals are usually linked to the store's computer and can help in ordering new stock for the supermarket. It can do this by letting the computer system know what goods have been sold in the store. (A detailed example is given in on page 91.)

Information about the goods that have been sold could be typed in by the operator but it is more convenient to read this

A

B

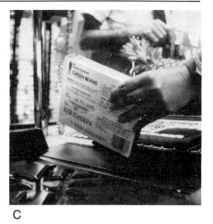

C

information from a *bar code* which is now found on most products.

The information contained in the bar code can be read by a *bar code reader* (sometimes called an *optical wand*). A typical bar code together with reader can be seen in Photograph B. It is often quicker and more convenient for the bar code to be read by a *laser scanner* and one is shown in Photograph C.

If the bar code is read, then no extra information need be fed in by the operator. All the information about the product is contained in the code. If the computer connected to the POS terminal knows the exact product that has been sold then it is possible for the computer to look up its current price list and send this price information back to the POS terminal. The customer can then have a receipt which not only contains the correct prices, but a detailed account of each item that has been sold.

Although very expensive, POS terminals mean that there will be fewer mistakes as less information has to be typed in. The queue should move more quickly as the information is entered using the bar code instead of typing, and the customer can also get a receipt which is generated automatically. It is very much easier for the store to change the price information and stock levels can be automatically monitored by the computer system.

Task

1   List three things that you think would be contained in the bar code information on the side of a can of baked beans.

Questions

2   What is meant by a POS terminal?
3   List three different ways in which data can be fed into a POS terminal at the checkout of a supermarket.
4   List four advantages of a POS terminal compared with a normal till in a small shop.
5   You have set up a chain of shops which run a mail-order business. People choose goods from a catalogue and then go to a branch of your shop where the goods can be picked up, or get them sent to them by post. List five ways in which a computer system in one of the shops may help the day-to-day running of the shop.

Home Computers

There are many applications of microcomputers in the home. From accessing information from viewdata and teletext systems, through computer learning packages in more subjects than many people care to think of, to entertainment and playing of adventure games. Microcomputers can play a greater number of roles than any other form of technology found in the home. Indeed, it is this versatility that makes the microcomputer a very difficult machine for some people to come to terms with and understand.

Fortunately, we do not have to understand very much about computers to use them in many worthwhile situations in the home. The professionals have spent many thousands of hours writing software that enable computers to be used very easily by non-specialist people. Some examples of software packages that can be used in the home now follow.

Photograph A shows a typical package that you might buy in the shops. It enables you to draw pictures on your computer. Such a package may include:

1 Software (On disk or cassette)
2 Mouse (see below)
3 User's manual

When you open the box you will have to read the instructions very carefully. If the manual is good, it should explain how to plug in the mouse and how to start the program running.

A mouse is simply a piece of hardware that plugs into the computer to enable you to move around the screen without using the keyboard.

After loading the disk and typing in a simple command the program should present you with some useful information on the screen. In fact, sometimes this information on the screen is so helpful that you do not need to read the manual very much at all! Such programs are said to be user friendly. This is because they are easy and obvious to use even to a relative beginner.

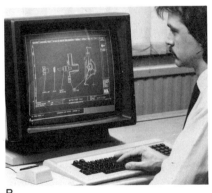

A

The particular package shown enables you to create pictures on the screen of the computer and print them out on a dot matrix printer if you are lucky enough to own one. An example of the mouse and what the screen may look like when the program is in use is shown in Photograph B.

The above program is an example of Computer Aided Design (CAD). i.e. the computer was used as an aid to help you design a picture. More sophisticated CAD packages will be considered on page 74 covering industrial applications.

B

Task

Find out and make a list of the things that are necessary to run three different applications packages that you have at your school or college. Both hardware and software should be considered.

Games

If your home computer is used only to play games then you will probably find that it is not used at all after two or three years. This is because it has been treated like a toy with which you have become bored. However, games form an important and often interesting part of the home microcomputer market. On some of the computers the latest games are very sophisticated.

Over the last few years the graphics capability of home microcomputers have increased by enormous amounts. Only several years ago you were limited to black and white, or, at most, seven or eight different colours. Today, on the most expensive home micros, up to 512 different colours are possible, with pictures in detail never dreamed of before. As an example, the adventure game called 'The Pawn', running on an Atari 520 ST computer can be seen in Photograph C.

C

Eventually, with the arrival of the video disk, video quality moving images will make games very much more realistic.

Task

1 Look at two different types of computer games. Make a list of the keys that are used to control various operations within the game.

Questions

2 Which of the following applications could not be satisfactorily carried out by a home computer and why?
   a) Playing a game of chess.
   b) Babysitting.
   c) Controlling the central heating.
   d) Home banking.
   e) Playing music.
3 It is not necessary to understand very much about computers to run a good program that has been written by someone else. Why is this?
4 In a recent survey, it was found that complete beginners often took several hours to get their new home computer system to do anything useful. Often they could not make it do anything at all! Suggest some reasons for this.
5 Computer games are now becoming more realistic. Some people think that in the future, a computer game might involve putting people into a chamber, where it would appear to the person playing the game, that they were in another world. What sort of things inside the chamber do you think coukd be controlled by the computer? Do you think that this is really likely to happen? If not, why?

Computer Aided Learning

Computer Aided Learning or CAL as it is known is the name given to the process of using computers to teach various subjects. As the hardware is becoming more sophisticated, and the software packages written in a more imaginative way, learning by computer is becoming a very pleasurable way to learn.

There are many advantages of CAL. Students can learn at their own pace, the computer never gets bored and never tires of asking many similar questions. A well written CAL package should be able to cope with the user typing in silly information. Sometimes, on badly written CAL packages, the program will stop working properly if you type in something ridiculous. If this happens, the program is said to have *crashed* and will have to be started again.

However, the computer can't cope with every situation and the student may find that they need the help of a teacher at certain points. As with computer games, the use of a video disk will enable moving video quality pictures to be used with the computer asking the questions. For example, you can imagine the computer presenting the user with a picture of some fine work of art and asking various questions about the artist or the painting.

You can also imagine the computer being used in foreign language tuition. This will really be useful when computer speech becomes more advanced and acceptable.

Tasks

If you have a CAL package available, use it and give your opinion of the following:

1 Is the manual easy to use?
2 Is the package user friendly?
3 Does the program crash if silly data is typed in?
4 How long did it take for you to get the program running?
5 Did you need any help from your teacher in using the program?

(NOTE You should use packages that you have never seen before, and get little or no help from a teacher or anyone who knows how to operate it.)

Computers in Commerce

Word processing

This is one of the most important commercial applications and has revolutionised the office of today. Word processors are really the computer-age's answer to typewriters; but with a difference. However, it is this difference which makes them so incredibly powerful. Even the simplest of word processors far out perform the most sophisticated electronic typewriters. As the cost of the typewriter is often more than the word processor, the days of the typewriter as a sensible machine on which to process text are numbered. Occasionally you buy a machine which is a dedicated word processor. i.e. it can't do anything else. However, the trend today is to buy a microcomputer and an appropriate software package which turns your computer into a word processor. Used in this way, you have the added advantage that the computer can do many other things. However, it must be said that if you want the most sophisticated facilities then a special 'word processor only' machine might be necessary.

To get an appreciation of what a word processor can do you must use one. Part of your course should involve a considerable amount of work using a word processor. There is not enough space to concentrate on the details of any particular word processor, you will find this information in the user manual. However, you need to know what sort of things that can be done with them.

Text entry mode

When you start the word processor and enter *text mode*, what you type in at the keyboard appears on the screen. As an example, let us consider the following paragraph of text:

```
This is  just a very short  paragraph  of text that
has been typed  into a  word  processor to show you
some of the  sophisticated things that  can be done
with word processors. You must  concentrate on what
is being  said and the  effect that  it has on this
text.
```

The first thing that you will notice with most word processors is that the text is automatically lined up so that each side of the text is straight. This gives a professional business-like look to your letters. This process is called *justification*. If you don't want the word processor to automatically justify your text then you can instruct the word processor to stop doing it.

There are usually two modes to enter text: *insert* and *overwrite*. If you are in insert mode, then the text you are typing is inserted in between the other text. The text moves along just as if you are shunting trains. The other mode is overwrite. In this case the text you are typing in overwrites the old text. It no longer pushes the old text out of the way.

Even the above operations have far exceeded the capacity of some standard electronic typewriters. We have far exceeded the mechanical typewriter's capability already.

Altering the width of columns

One of the biggest advantages of word processors is that you type in the text without much thought, then get the word processor to lay it out exactly as you want by giving it special instructions.

As an example, let us assume that we are writing a column for a newspaper. The original text could be laid out so that each line is 50 characters long.

Now the text has been typed in as:

```
This is just a very short  paragraph  of text that
has been typed  into a word  processor to show you
some of the  sophisticated things that can be done
with word processors. You must concentrate on what
is being said and the  effect that  it has on this
text.
```

However, after a simple command to tell the word processor to lay out the text again but this time using only 30 characters per line we get:

```
This   is   just   a   very short
paragraph   of   text   that has
been    typed    into    a   word
processor to show you some of
the sophisticated things that
can   be   done   with    word
processors.          You     must
concentrate  on   what is being
said  and  the   effect that   it
has on this   text.
```

Notice that the text has now been laid out as requested. The word processor has done this by inserting extra spaces in between the words. The fourth line from the bottom shows the method most clearly.

Many highly skilled and highly paid people in the newspaper industry used to spend their days laying out text in columns like the example shown above. The same results can now be achieved with a word processor and an unskilled person in a few seconds. This is a good example of a skilled person's job being taken over by a computer.

Command mode

When you have entered the text and laid it out exactly to your specification it is then possible to do many other sophisticated things in command mode. In this mode, you can issue commands to the word processor to do things such as find words, replace words with others, check spelling or generate an index. As an example of one of these processes consider the REPLACE command: The original text is:

```
This is  just a very short  paragraph  of text that
has been typed  into  a  word  processor to show you
some of the  sophisticated  things that can be  done
with word processors. You  must concentrate on  what
is being  said and the  effect that  it has on  this
text.
```

Suppose that from command mode on a particular word processor we type:

```
FIND /word processor/ REPLACE /beefburger/
```

After typing return you would find the text altered to the following:

```
This is just a very short  paragraph  of text that
has  been  typed  into  a  beefburger  to show you
some of the  sophisticated  things that can be done
with  beefburgers.  You  must  concentrate on  what
is being said and the  effect that  it has on  this
text.
```

Notice that every occurrence of the words 'word processor' have been replaced with the word 'beefburger'.

It is unlikely that anyone would want to replace 'word processor' with 'beefburger' but it demonstrates the principle. You can imagine Febuary having to be replaced with February (i.e. the correct spelling).

Standard letters

Another big advantage for the office is the generation of *standard letters*. Often business people have to send out the same type of letters to many different customers. For example, a company may decide to send out a personalised Christmas greeting to all their customers thanking them for their custom and wishing them a Happy New Year.

It is possible for the word processor to make use of the business files, find the names and addresses of the customers, and then automatically generate the letter to each customer.

Not only can the word processor generate the letters but often they can address the envelopes as well! You can even send the text by electronic mail if you so wish.

There are many things that word processors can do. We have mentioned only very few of them above. If you can use and understand them very well, you will not wish to produce text using any other method.

Questions

1 What is a word processor?
2 List three things that can be done more easily on a word processor than a typewriter.
3 State three things that can be done with text on a word processor after the text has been entered.
4 What is meant by a standard letter? Why are standard letters particularly suitable for word processing?

Payroll Systems

One of the first commercial uses of computers was to calculate the wages of people who worked in companies. You can imagine that it is time consuming, tedious and boring for people to have to work out the wages for thousands of others each week. It is a process which is ideal for computerisation.

Inputs to the system

Collection of data is obviously important because it is vital to find out how many hours different people have worked so that they get the correct amount of money. There is nothing worse than not being paid enough. Nobody complains if they are paid too much!

It is usual for data to be collected from clock cards or time sheets. Clock cards are cards that are placed into special machines that punch the time directly onto the card in *machine readable form*. i.e. the clock cards can then be fed into the computer system.

If the employee submits a time sheet then it is usual for data entry staff to type in the times for each employee into the system via a keyboard.

As the data to be entered must be 100% correct if possible, it is usually verified before being used in the main payroll program. In addition to this verification process, the data must be validated at appropriate points during the main processing. For example, checks must be made to make sure that an employee has not worked 35 hours in any one day, etc.!

The main processing

The computer must have access to certain information about each employee if it is to be able to calculate their net pay (i.e. the pay that they take home). It does this by making deductions from their gross pay. (The amount they earn.) Such deductions will be *tax*, *national insurance*, *company pension schemes* etc. Information to enable the computer to do this is usually found on special files.

The following files are needed by the payroll system.

Master file

The system will usually have a *master file* which contains all the names and addresses of each employee. This could be alphabetical but it is more likely to be sorted by *employee number*. This is to avoid the possibility of two people having the same name and initials getting mixed up.

In addition the master file contains information such as the employee *tax code* (i.e. a code which the computer uses to know how much tax to deduct), *hourly rate* (the amount of pay for each hour) and other similar information which would be needed.

Transaction file

This will be made up of all the verified data that has either been directly input to the system or typed in. It is most likely that this transaction file will have to be sorted into employee number order before getting it ready to be used in the pay run.

Other files

In addition to the above two files, special files such as *tax tables* will also be needed. These are modified from time to time if the tax rate changes or if allowances are altered.

Processing programs

The payroll software will probably consist of several programs called a *suite of programs*. Some of the programs will calculate the gross pay from the input data, others will update the master files and others will generate the pay slips ready to be put inside the pay packets.

In addition to the above the employer will want an account of how much wages have been paid, how much has to be paid to the inland revenue or how much each person has paid into the pension scheme etc.

The only way to get an overall view of a typical payroll system is to look at a typical *systems flowchart*. One is shown in Diagram A.

Notice that the system flowchart symbols described on page 47 have been used.

It should be realised that batch processing is most suitable for payroll applications. It is likely, that if the workforce is to be paid on Friday, then the payroll program would be run on Wednesday or Thursday evening. Most people are paid one week behind.

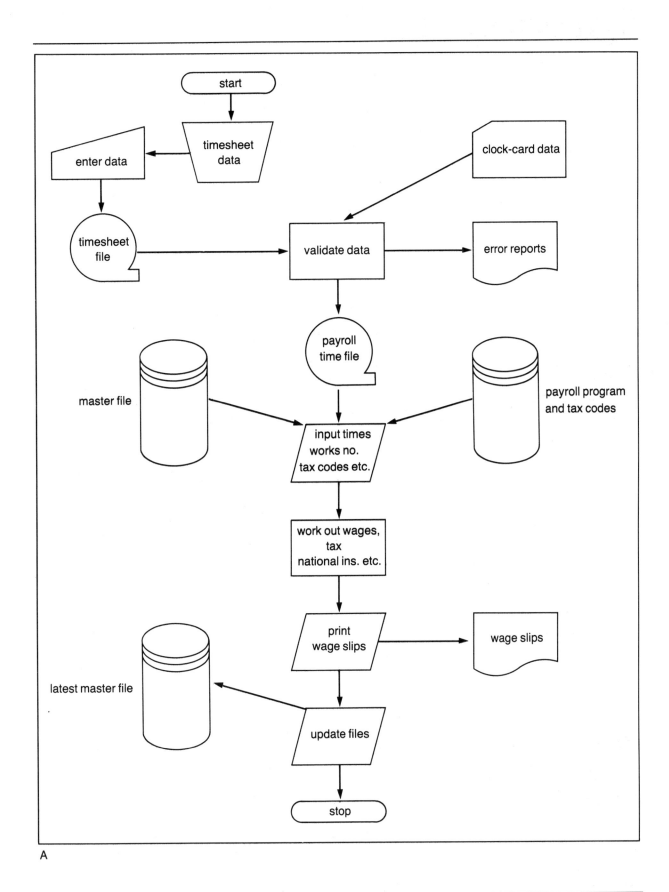

A

1 What inputs are there likely to be to a payroll processing program?
2 Why is batch processing more suitable for payroll applications?
3 Name two processes that the payroll transaction file would normally go through before being used to calculate the wages.

Spreadsheets

This is an application which is just as important to businesses as word processors. In fact, *spreadsheets* are so useful that often microcomputers are sold just to be used as a spreadsheet.

A spreadsheet can easily answer typical business-type questions like what would happen to profits if cost of raw materials rise by 5% but interest rates fall by 3%? Although these would be simple calculations, similar questions when more things change can take hours to work out by hand, even with a calculator. A spreadsheet can give you the answers in seconds.

To be able to fully appreciate the power of a spreadsheet you should use one. However, the principles are simple and will now be explained.

What is a spreadsheet?

Spreadsheets can be very large indeed having many rows and columns, but we will consider a small one in this example.

A spreadsheet consists of *rows* and *columns* as shown in Diagram A.

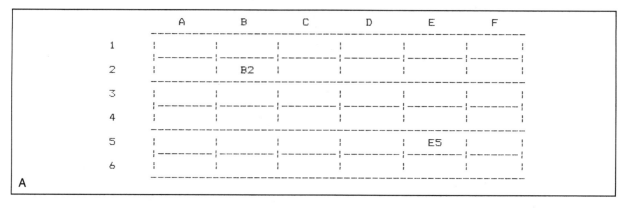

The little boxes that are formed are called *cells*. Cells B2 and E5 are shown in the above example.

How does a spreadsheet operate?

Suppose that we run a business which deals in the manufacture of garden sheds. The raw materials that go into making each shed are as follows:

Full Description	Abbreviation	Quantity	Cost/Unit
Wood for the walls in 3 m lengths.	Wood	120	1.20
Window frames.	Wind	2	15.20
Glass for the windows.	Glass	4	7.30
Felt for the roof.	Felt	2	12.75
Nuts and bolts to join the shed.	Nu/Bo	90	0.30
Creosote to preserve the wood.	Creo	1	1.75
Fixtures for the windows.	Fixw	2	6.90
Fixtures for the door.	Fixd	1	8.90

The full description gives the materials used, and the abbreviations show how these materials are to be described in the spreadsheets. Also, the quantity and price per unit are shown in the last two columns.

For example, if you wanted to know how much the wood costs for the shed you need 120 units at £1.20 for each unit which gives a total of £144 for the wood.

In addition to the raw materials costs, labour costs are as follows:

Workers are paid £3.90 per hour.
It takes nine hours to build a shed.

Now the price of the raw materials vary from month to month, and so we need to know what effect this is going to have on our profits. Similarly, what if the workers ask for an 8% rise? How will this affect the final cost of the shed etc.?

Filling in the spreadsheet

To answer the above sort of questions we must enter the relevant information into the computer so that the spreadsheet is built up. This has only to be done once and is shown in Diagram B.

	A	B	C	D	E	F
1	WOOD	120	1.20			
2	WIND	2	15.20			
3	GLASS	4	7.30			
4	FELT	2	12.75			
5	NU/BO	90	0.30			
6	CREA	1	1.75			
7	FIXW	2	6.90			
8	FIXD	1	8.90			
9	LAB	9	4.90			
10			TOTAL			

B

The above is simply a copy of the table on page 68. It would be easy to work out the next column manually. All that is necessary is to multiply the two previous columns together. However, this would defeat the object of using the computer. We must therefore, tell the computer how to work it out for us.

Calculations

To get the total cost of the wood, we *multiply* the number in *cell* B1 by the number in *cell* C1 and put the *answer* in *cell* D1.

We write this as $D1 = B1 \times C1$

Also, $\qquad D2 = B2 \times C2$

and $\qquad D3 = B3 \times C3$ etc.

In fact, for our shed, all the formulae are very similar, but on more complex spreadsheets long calculations are just as easily done.

The only different type formula in our example occur when dealing with cell D10. This is the cell which is going to contain the total cost for the shed. This is obtained by adding all the figures in the column:

i.e. $D10 = D1 + D2 + D3 + D4 + D5 + D6 + D7 + D8 + D9$

When we have entered all the formulae into the spreadsheet we can press a key to get the computer to work out the total cost for the shed. This would produce the spreadsheet shown in Diagram C.

	A	B	C	D	E	F
1	WOOD	120	1.20	144.00		
2	WIND	2	15.20	30.40		
3	GLASS	4	7.30	29.20		
4	FELT	2	12.75	25.50		
5	NU/BO	90	0.30	2.70		
6	CREA	1	1.75	1.75		
7	FIXW	2	6.90	13.80		
8	FIXD	1	8.90	8.90		
9	LAB	9	3.90	35.10		
10			TOTAL	291.35		

C

It would be easy to add a further row which allowed for £50 profit. If added, then the label in cell C11 would be *profit* and the formula to work out D11 would be:

$$D11 = D10 + 50.00$$

Also, we could add a *cost to customer* row. The final two rows would look something like:

	A	B	C	D	E	F
10			TOTAL	291.35		
11			PROFIT	50.00		
12			COST	341.35		

Using the spreadsheet

Having entered all the data we can now make use of the spreadsheet. For example, what would happen to the total cost if labour costs rise by 20%?

All we have to do is to change £3.90 in cell C9 to £4.68 to reflect the 20% rise. We then instruct the computer to do all the calculations again and we instantly get the answer:

	A	B	C	D	E	F
9	LAB	9	4.68	42.12		
10			TOTAL	298.37		
11			PROFIT	50.00		
12			COST	348.37		

Although the above was simple, you can see that in a large business with many different materials going into making many different products, spreadsheets are a most useful timesaver for doing long and tedious arithmetic.

Spreadsheets take all the hard work out of calculating how much profit and so on is made. Management can now use spreadsheets to recalculate things that would have taken a long time when done manually.

Questions

1 Why are spreadsheets so useful in business?
2 Give an example of the sort of things that can be done easily with a spreadsheet that was time consuming to do by hand.
3 You are starting a business and want to use spreadsheets to help work out your finances. Choose only *one* of the following and make a list of most of the things that you think ought to be included on a spreadsheet.

a) Decorating houses.
b) Making dresses.
c) Building coffee tables.
d) Running a computer advice-shop.

Computers in Industry

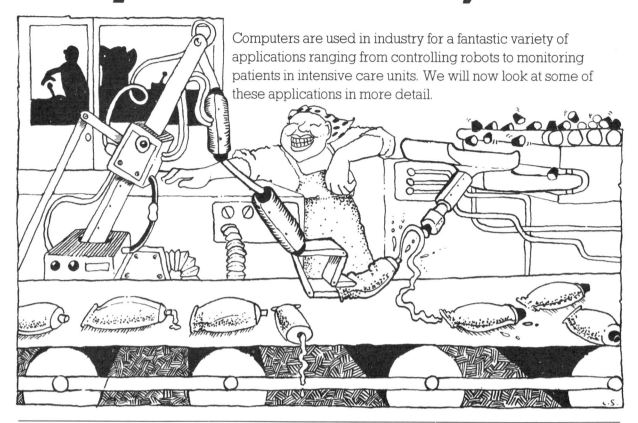

Computers are used in industry for a fantastic variety of applications ranging from controlling robots to monitoring patients in intensive care units. We will now look at some of these applications in more detail.

Robotics

The first thing to make clear is that *industrial robots* do not look anything like humans, nor are they meant to be like humans in any way. They are usually designed for a single task that they perform twenty-four hours a day, seven days a week. Some typical robots performing their tasks are shown in Photograph A.

A

B

C

D

Photograph A shows a robot welding a car body, Photograph B shows a robot hand holding a glass. Photograph C shows a robot working with bomb disposal and finally, Photograph D shows a robot moving material from one part of a factory to another.

It is important to realise that the glass holding robot could not possibly weld the car together as each are designed for a very special purpose. However, there are more general-purpose robots which can be programmed by computer to do different things. These tend to be educational robot arms or toy robots designed to mimic human behaviour. However, they can't do lots of different things as well as robots that are designed for specific tasks.

Robots can have several advantages. They can go into places which would be dangerous for humans, e.g. too much radiation or heat, or they can work for many hours without stopping. They can also do very humdrum tasks without getting bored. However, they are not as versatile as humans and can't be programmed to do very different jobs easily.

The art of using robots is to use them for doing jobs at which they are more efficient than humans. They can work alongside humans who can do the more interesting and varied tasks.

Questions

1 Why can't robots do a variety of tasks?
2 Give a situation where robots can work where humans could not.
3 Why has the domestic robot that can do all the housework not caught on yet?
4 What is meant by an industrial robot?
5 Give three different types of work that robots can do.

Computer Aided Design

Computers are often used to help designers visualise what they are going to build. For example, when designing aircraft or cars, it is vary useful to get the computer to simulate what the designer will see from many different angles. A typical computer aided design (CAD) terminal would have a very large screen and one can be seen in Photograph A.

Devices called *light pens* are often used to point to areas of interest on the screen so that parts of the design may be enlarged or drawn out in more detail. The computer can also be used to run calculations on things such as the wind resistance of a car before it is even built. In this way, expensive and time consuming model building is only started at a much later stage in the design cycle, after the designs have been tested by computer.

A

B

CAD systems are often essential. Without them some jobs would be impossible. For example, the inside of microprocessor chips are now so complex that it would be virtually impossible for people to draw them without making a mistake. Therefore, computers are now used to help to design the next generation of computers. A typical system is shown in Photograph B.

Computer aided management (CAM)

We have already seen how word processors can help secretaries and how spreadsheets can help accountants. There are many other software packages that are designed to help managers make better decisions by processing complex information that would not be easy without computers.

A typical example of CAM will be given to show how one system called *critical path analysis* is used.

Critical path analysis

Suppose that you were in charge of planning and progress on a very large building site for a major hospital. Much thought must be given to making sure that the right people are available on the building site at the right time, and that all the appropriate materials are ready for them to use.

Examples of the people you would be controlling are engineers, bricklayers, carpenters, plumbers, lorry drivers, surveyors, planners, inspectors and site foreman. Can you imagine how complex a task it would be to make sure that the right materials were delivered on time, the right people were at the site at the right time, and no delays held up the project? It is almost certain that you will have a deadline to meet when the health authority expect the hospital to be opened.

Computer programs have been written that enable you to enter and plan all the processes that have to be carried out. Each job is split up into separate tasks such as clearing the site, digging the hole for the foundations, laying the foundations, building the external framework etc. Towards the end of the construction you will need to paint and decorate and perhaps install some of the large items of medical equipment such as X-ray machines.

The computer system will enable you to enter each task along with the materials that are needed, the amount of time that the task is expected to take, the people needed for the task, and the position of the task within the plan. i.e. what things need to be done before a particular task can be carried out.

It is then possible to get the computer to estimate a time when either special parts of the project will be complete, or when the whole project will be completed. The computer will highlight any paths through all the jobs that need special attention if the project is to be completed on time. These paths are known as *critical paths* because they are critical if the project is to be completed by the desired date.

CAM to decorate your front room?

As an example of a very simple problem consider decorating the front room of your house. The processes that need to be done are:

Remove or cover up the furniture and carpets.
Choosing the paper and paint.
Stripping of the old paper and preparing the walls.
Rubbing down the old paint.
Putting on the undercoat and leaving it to dry.
Putting on the top coat and leaving it to dry.
Putting up the new paper.
Remove covers or bring back furniture and carpets.

The above are not necessarily in the order in which each task would have to be carried out. For example, choosing the paper and paint could be done before removing the furniture.

Diagram C shows these tasks set out in a way that could be entered into a computer.

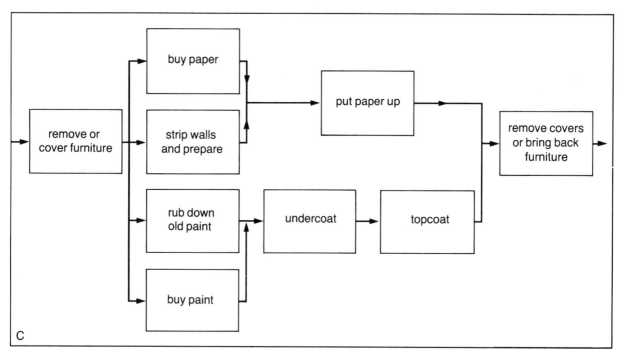

C

The time for each task is then written under each box. The *longest path* through the project must be the critical path because the project will not be completed until this is done. Therefore, any tasks in this critical path will have to be done as quickly as possible. If the project had to be completed in a shorter time, then a person could be taken off one of the tasks that are not critical and put on one of the tasks that is. In the above example, it is not necessary to go out and buy the paper until the preparation and painting has been done. Paper could be bought while waiting for the paint to dry.

Although the above example is simple, you can see how such help from computers would make projects like large scale building construction more manageable by using computer aided management techniques.

Tasks

1 Make a list of the things that need to be done when going on holiday.

   For example:
   book tickets, check passports if necessary, get the sun tan oil etc.

2 From your list choose three things that would delay your holiday if these things were not satisfactory.

3 You are in charge of a firm that is trying to sell software that helps people to manage large projects. You have a customer who is interested in building a bridge across a river. Explain to them how your computer system can help them to get the project finished on time.

Computers in Control

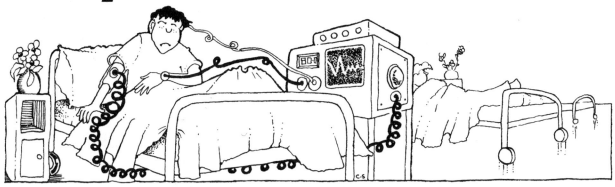

Hospitals

There are often situations where a process needs constant monitoring. For example, a patient in an intensive care ward. Computers can be connected to special electronic devices so that physical effects such as heart rate, temperature and blood pressure, can all be monitored.

Suppose that in a large hospital there are fifteen patients in an intensive care ward. It would take fifteen nurses to monitor each patient constantly. However, they could all be easily monitored by a single computer. A single nurse could then cope by responding to any alarms that the computer might sound if a patient's condition becomes critical.

A typical system would probably have a central control unit which would ring bells and an appropriate light to indicate which patient is in danger.

The intensive care system is more reliable when controlled by computer as the computer does not get bored when constantly monitoring several things twenty-four hours a day.

Power stations

Another situation where constant monitoring of important data is necessary is in the power industry. It is essential that if anything should go wrong, such as a leak in a cooling pipe or a faulty pump then the heat producing system must be closed down immediately.

If humans were left to monitor the situation then they would get very bored indeed. Imagine sitting down all day looking at a few dials. You would almost certainly fall asleep!

Traffic light control

Traffic jams in London are a constant problem. Everybody has complained about them at one stage or another. However, have you ever thought what would happen if all the traffic lights failed. Many traffic lights in central London are controlled from the large computer system shown in Photograph A.

A

In addition to switching the lights on and off, the computers monitor the flow and build up of traffic. This data is automatically picked up by electronic sensors placed at strategic positions. When this data has been fed into the computer it is analysed so that each set of lights may be red or green for just the right amount of time necessary to keep the traffic flowing as smoothly as possible.

It is often the case that traffic will be heavier in certain directions at various times of the day. For example, in the morning rush hour most people are trying to get into London, but during the evening rush hour, most people are trying to get out of London. Therefore, the traffic lights have different priorities at different times during the day.

Also, parts of the system may be manually controlled to allow for situations such as accidents etc. TV cameras are placed at special positions to allow the police to look at the current traffic situation.

Questions

1 Give four different applications where computers are used to control industrial processes.
2 Why are computers better than people at constantly monitoring things?
3 Give a situation where a person would be much better than a computer when controlling an application.
4 Give some applications where it would be impossible for a process to be done were it not computer controlled.
5 You are a member of the government and have been given the job of convincing the unions in a large car manufacturing plant that they must have a new automated production line. What arguments would you use to convince them?

Data Base Applications

One of the largest applications of computers today is the storing and manipulation of huge amounts of data. Some of the methods of extracting data from these systems are extremely sophisticated making it possible to get information about a huge variety of topics very easily. Such systems have come to be known as *data bases*.

If you have used filing systems on a computer before you will realise that only a limited amount of information can be obtained from any one file. For example, consider the administration computer in a typical school. Such a system may have much information stored for specific purposes.

If 'names and addresses' are required then the file containing this information will have to be used. Similarly, if the subjects that pupils are studying at school are required, then another file will have to be loaded. It is possible, that the same system could be used the get both items of information. If this were possible, then it would be easy to combine the information to get extra information from the computer. For example, it would be possible to print out the names and addresses of all the pupils who are studying geography in the fourth form. This may be very useful for the geography teacher if a trip is to be planned.

Task

List several things that are usually stored on a computer at school. Using your list, outline three examples where combinations of information would be useful, and the people who would make use of such information.

What is a data base?

A data base is the name given to a system (usually quite complicated) that consists of many files of information. You would be right in thinking that a computer system can consist of lots of files but the main thing that is different about a data base is that all the files can interact with each other. this allows people to be able to extract useful information from the data base according to individual needs as shown in the example above.

If you have a data base system in your school or college then find out how it is possible to make enquiries of the above sort. It is usual to use what is called a *query language*. A typical example of a query language is now given.

Suppose that you have a data base that is set up to store information for use in a dating agency. Let us assume that the following is a typical example of some of the information stored in one of the files for the London area.

```
            Example                 Possible Entries
            Name              S. B. Bradley
            Address           23, Barbados Terrace, London
            Age               24
            Sex               Female            Male/Female
            Hair colour       Fair              Fair/Dark
            Height            Medium            Short/Medium/Tall
            Character type    Indoor            Indoor/Outdoor
```

Many more things can obviously be said about suitable dating partners but the above will be used as a simple example. When using a query language, you can often use operations such as AND, OR, NOT, > (greater than), < (less than) and = to describe your ideal match.

Choosing your date!

For example, if you wanted to meet a female who was tall and aged between seventeen and twenty-one then you may write:

```
Query female: Age >17 and age <21 : height tall :
Print name and address
```

After typing out the above, all the names and addresses of the females who are tall, and aged between seventeen and twenty-one will have their names and addresses typed out by the data base. As you did not specify an area, all the files for all the areas in the country would be looked at. You may end up with quite a large list!

Task

1 Write down information that may be contained in a data base for use in a second-hand car sales showroom. i.e. to enable people to enquire about make, colour, engine capacity etc.

Questions

2 What is a data base?
3 Write down some of the files that might be needed in a data base held by the police for criminal investigations.
  For example files of stolen cars, files of people with prison records etc.
4 In question (3), suggest some files that might be used when the police investigate an armed bank robbery with a fast get away car.

External data bases

The data bases described above all had the information stored on your local computer. One of the most powerful things that computers can now do is to get information from other data bases that are held on computers in other parts of the country. One of the best examples is Prestel run by British Telecom. Here, it is possible to get information from a vast data base via the telephone system. The Prestel system has been described in detail on page 34.

There are many such data bases set up in the British Isles and even more throughout the world. To access information held on these data bases requires a detailed knowledge of what to type into the computer. This information should be found in the manuals for each system. However, it is much easier if you get your teacher to demonstrate such systems as it takes some time to get used to them.

The Problems of Standardisation

Computer systems have been introduced into the office and businesses with amazing speed. It has been worked out that in just five years after the introduction of the microcomputer these machines can be found in about 95% of offices.

The above may sound impressive but in practice sharing of information between one office and another or even between different computers in the same office has caused major problems.

In large businesses separate computer systems have often grown up in different departments. Each system would normally be ideally suited to a particular task. For example, the accounts department would have a computer system that is ideal for working out the accounts and payroll, and the secretaries would have ideal word processors etc.

The problem arises when information from the accounts computer is needed to be included in a document that is being produced on a word processor. Often, the only way to transfer the information between the accounts machine and the word processor is to print out the information from the accounts machine, and get the secretary to type it into the word processor! This is obviously a very inefficient way to run a computer system in a large business.

One of the reasons for the above problems is that no computer manufacturer has agreed on a standard method to be able to transfer information from one machine to another. The situation is improving however, and in a few years time we ought to see computer systems able to transfer information between themselves more easily.

One way to get round the problem now is to make use of electronic mail. You can send information from one computer down the telephone line to a mainframe with electronic mail facilities. Then, when the other incompatible computer wants to get the information it needs it can do so from the electronic mailbox of the mainframe.

The problems of incompatibility

Even computers made by the same manufacturer often have problems with transferring data between one machine and another. One example is the different sizes of floppy disks that are available. 8 inch, $5\frac{1}{4}$ inch and 3 inch are all 'standard'. A machine with a 3 inch floppy disk system, would not be able to save data on a disk suitable for a machine with a $5\frac{1}{4}$ inch disk system.

The problems are even worse than described above. Different versions of software even on the same type of computer often make it difficult or even impossible to get the same piece of software running!

Throughout your course you will be aware of these problems, especially if you use different types of computer systems.

Questions

1 Why is it not easy to connect one computer to another?
2 What problems arise from not being able to connect different computers?
3 How could some of these problems be overcome?
4 Do you think it would be a good idea to have a centralised national computer data base that contains a lot of personal information about all the people in the country? Write two arguments. One which is *for* and the other which is *against* the idea of a national data base.

The data base trend

One way to get over all the above problems is to have a centralised data base which stores all the information about the business. If these systems are cleverly written then any type of microcomputer with the correct software can access information from the data base.

Too much information?

Data bases must be very large to be of any use. For example, if you were doing a history project and wanted to know all the books that were available on some special topic then it would be useless if, when you searched a large library data base, many of the appropriate books were missing. Ideally, all the books published by all the publishers everywhere in the world ought to be on such a data base.

Data bases are searched in a way similar to that described in the computer dating system on page 80. Imagine that you were doing a project about the Second World War. It should be possible to ask the computer controlling the data base to give you a list of all the books that have been printed about the Second world War! Unfortunately, hundreds if not thousands of titles would be printed!

You will therefore have to be more specific in your request. Perhaps you could ask for all the books to be listed which cover 1943 to 1944. This would however still produce a very long list.

The trouble is that the computer needs to know exactly the sort of information that you are looking for. It is a pity that most data bases today do not think like human beings. For example, if you asked a librarian to help you with the problem she would realise that you were at school and doing a GCSE history project, she would therefore immediately discount many books that would, in her opinion be too advanced or too simple. She would ask you further questions about your project and guide you by asking more specific details as you go along.

Intelligent data bases

One of the latest trends is to build this sort of intelligence into a data base by using artificial intelligence techniques. This is only in the development stage but it should make data bases react to give a more sensible output when you request information.

Computer People

There are many different jobs in the computer industry, and people at all levels of skill and experience are needed. We will now look in detail at some of the tasks that these different people do.

Large or small computer

In a very small business the jobs that people do are very different from those who work for a large company. We will first concentrate on the large businesses as the tasks that people do in larger companies are much easier to define.

People who work with large computers

A large computer installation refers to a mainframe, or at least a large minicomputer. A large computer in this range will require many people to run and maintain it, and lots of other people to help feed data into it etc. There are also many jobs behind the scenes, especially if the company develops its own software, or is a computer manufacturer.

The computer operator

Large computer systems usually run twenty-four hours a day, seven days a week. They will normally provide a service to many people in the company and, very likely, to other people in other parts of the country via telephone communications or networks. Such a system requires that people are available to put paper in the printers, make sure that the correct disks are available to the computer and generally to make sure that the system is operating normally and the correct jobs are run. These people are called computer operators. The whole computer system is controlled by the computer operators typing in special instructions at a keyboard.

As the computer room is operating for most of the day and night, computer operators are normally required to work shifts. In a very large computer installation there would be two or three operators and a *shift leader* who is in charge for that shift.

The data preparation staff

In a large department it is an enormous task to make sure that all the data is entered into the system properly. Often many typists are required to operate the key-to-disk or key-to-tape machines. It is also usual to have a person in charge of this important department. They are called the *data preparation supervisor*.

In addition to simply typing in the data, it is the job of this department to collect the data, verify it and sort out any errors that have been detected.

Systems analysts

If a company wants to computerise, to update their existing system or simply to add one or two extra facilities to their old one, it is usual to call in some expert help. The person, (or group of people), in charge of sorting out these complicated problems are called *systems analysts*. They are highly trained and experienced people with a great deal of knowledge about computer systems and applications.

If the job that they are tackling is quite large, then it would normally take many months for detailed studies to be carried out. However, at the end of this analysis phase, a plan will have been worked out on how to proceed with the task.

Occasionally, the systems analyst will recommend that a computer is not needed! They may say that the best way to do the task is by some other method. This could save the company wasting much money on an expensive computer system that would not really help them with their problems.

The systems analysts don't usually write any programs, they would simply explain what programs would be be needed and draw up systems flowcharts to show other people how the system operates.

Programmers

It is the job of *computer programmers* to take instructions from the systems analyst. Using these detailed instructions, they will then write programs. It would be very unusual for one programmer to write all the programs that are necessary for a complete system. A team of programmers is usually given this task under the supervision of a chief programmer. It is most important that all the programmers work together and agree on how things need be done. Compare this situation with writing your own programs at school. It is very different indeed.

One of the major tasks of programmers in industry is to update systems when this becomes necessary. It is often the case that the people who wrote the original programs are no longer present, and therefore a new person must take on the task of modifying someone else's program. This is why it is essential for the person who originally wrote the program to supply a detailed set of instructions explaining how it works. Without this documentation, it is often very difficult if not impossible to modify a program.

The data processing manager

This is the person who is in charge of all the people mentioned above. The job would be a management one and they would rarely get involved in details about running the computer system. However, they would be very much involved with the progress that projects were making, and in the development of new projects. They would be the people who hire and fire staff and sort out any disputes that may arise between different departments etc.

The small computer system

In a small business there may be several microcomputers or even only one. It is usually the responsibility of one person to look after the system, develop new ways of doing things, buy software or write their own, and manage the day-to-day running of the computers.

We can see from the above that a single person might be computer operator, data entry staff, systems analyst, programmer and data processing manager all rolled into one. This may seem like a tall order, but it is usually not as bad as it sounds, because the computer is not processing anywhere near the vast quantity of information that a large system would. Also, for the right person, doing all the above jobs can be extremely satisfying, especially when you see a project right through from start to finish.

Questions

1 Briefly explain the jobs of the following computer people:

a) computer operator,
b) data preparation staff,
c) systems analyst,
d) computer programmer,
e) data processing manager.

2 What is the main difference between the jobs of people looking after mainframe computers and microcomputers?
3 Name the job of a person in the computer industry who may have to work shifts.
4 What is the job of shift leader?
5 Name the job of a person who would be in charge of data preparation staff, programmers and systems analysts.

Trends in Computing

The speed with which computers have come to play important roles in the modern world is astounding. No other development of technology has had such an impact so quickly. The computer was invented in the form we know it today in the 1950s. Therefore, in less than 50 years, it has become a vital part of everybody's life.

You do not have to own a computer to be involved with them. If you own a car, get paid, go to hospital, buy food from a supermarket, watch TV, or simply go to school then you will have been affected by the introduction of the computer.

One of the remarkable things about computers is their ability to do a great variety of things. All you have to do is change the program and you have changed your word processor into a video games machine. Never before in history has a single machine been capable of performing such a variety of jobs. Add to this the ability of a computer to do several million things in a second, the fact that powerful microcomuter systems often cost less than a domestic cooker, use only about as much electricity as a light bulb and need very little attention: you can see that we have invented a truly amazing machine that can be purchased by almost anybody.

Some problems

The introduction of the computer has not been without problems: not least the problem of people either liking them or hating them! Very few other machines bring out emotions in people more than computers. However, when people understand computers they usually think they are a good thing if used properly. It is lack of understanding together with wild reports in the press and over the top science fiction movies that give the general public the impression they have of computers today. Hopefully, after completing your computer awareness course you will not be one of the many people who live in ignorance and fear of computers.

Employment

One of the main arguments against the introduction of computers is that people will lose their jobs. Although this is very true, unfortunately it is not an argument which will keep people in work if industry fails to computerise. This is because it is normally more efficient and cost effective to introduce computers into factories and offices. If you are more efficient, then the goods that you produce will cost less. If you do not computerise then your competitors abroad will be able to sell the same goods that your company makes at a much cheaper price. Therefore, the jobs that you thought would have been saved would be lost anyway.

The world is rapidly being split up into nations where labour is very cheap (such as Taiwan), and nations where labour is very expensive (such as the USA and Britain). This unfortunately means that we can no longer manufacture goods which need a large amount of labour to make them. The only way to remain competitive is to computerise and use robots or literally go bust.

The situation is not quite as bleak as it sounds because there will be many new jobs available in the computer-related industries. However, these are different types of jobs and people will need to be retrained in the new technologies. It is an unfortunate fact of life that not as many people will be needed as before. This means that there will be more people unemployed and problems such as unemployment will, I think, never go away. One of the ways of reducing unemployment to more acceptable levels is to boost other industries like the leisure industry. This is because as people have more time on their hands they will need places to go to be entertained and activities to do which they will enjoy. Indeed the tourist industry in Britain is one of the major growth areas and looks set to continue expanding for many years to come.

It is also true that computerisation does not necessarily mean that everyone's job will go. Many people will have to learn to do the same jobs in different ways. For example, in the office, word processors, electronic mail, spreadsheets and data bases are now a normal part of life. Only a few years ago the same jobs were being done by typewriters, postmen, masses of filing clerks using filing cabinets, accountants and general office workers. The same jobs are still there but less people are needed to do them due to the increased efficiency of the people who remain.

Questions

1 Name five different jobs where computers are used.
2 Why do some people lose their jobs when a company computerises?
3 Why are some people scared of computers?

Computers and Privacy

When personal and private data is stored there will always be problems with some unauthorised people trying to get the information. This problem has always been with us but the techniques needed in the past have been quite different from the high-tech techniques needed today.

Some examples now follow:

The burglar

Twenty or thirty years ago information in most offices would have been manually recorded on record cards inside filing cabinets. Indeed much information is still stored in this way today.

Now suppose that someone wanted to steal some information, they would have to break into and enter the building, find the appropriate office, break into the office, find the appropriate filing cabinet, force it open, and steal the file. They would then have to get out of the building undetected. Devices like burglar alarms and security systems would have to be overcome and a quick getaway at some unearthly hour during the middle of the night would be needed.

There is no doubt in the minds of the public that the above person is a thief, and a burglar. Everyone would agree that the culprit should be found and punished. However, consider the next example.

The executive

A top computer executive arrives at work at 9 a.m. He logs on to his computer system and uses a code that he has obtained to enter another computer illegally. He searches a data base and prints out information on his computer.

To the people around him the executive has been getting on with his work. In fact, he has obtained the same information that the burglar obtained in the example above. Both people have set out and committed the same sort of crime, but the methods today are a little different.

How to increase protection of data

The increase in computer networks using the telephone system has led to the biggest problems of all as illustrated by the second example given above. Therefore ways to increase the difficulty of getting unauthorised data have been developed.

We have already mentioned pass codes and user numbers at other points in this book. Indeed this would be enough to deter the casual browser who did not want to spend very much time or any money trying to get information. You will never have 100% security while there are people forming part of the system. This is because these people can be bribed into giving out classified information to others. Indeed this is the most common method which produces breaches of security.

The electronic solution

Assuming that you do have reliable people working in the computer room then it is still possible for other people to intercept and decode information from your system. This is especially true if it is transmitted over the telephone system. One way of getting over this is to use what is called *encryption devices*. These devices perform complex changes in the data so that even if anyone receives the data, then without the appropriate electronic key they could not decode it.

Today it is possible to produce a code that is so complex that it would take a supercomputer millions of years to decode it. However, some people have thought of banning the use of these very secure devices because even people like the police or Government agencies could not crack any of the codes!

Breaches in security

One does hear about cases in the press where information has been obtained illegally from computer systems. However, if the truth were known very many more cases are not even mentioned. This is because the companies would be embarrassed to admit that their security had been breached. For example, suppose you were a large bank: would you announce that half a million pounds could not be accounted for by your computer system? The loss of confidence by your customers would far outweigh the half million pounds that we have mentioned.

The situation gets even more bizarre. There are examples quoted where employees have been caught stealing money in this way. The individuals are usually so clever that they are not actually sacked, but employed again, this time in the security department! On a drastically increased salary of course.

Questions

1 Why do computers make it easy for some people to obtain information illegally?
2 What can be done to increase security on computer systems?
3 Why can computers never be 100% secure?
4 You have a friend who thinks he is a 'computer whiz-kid' because he can write a few complicated BASIC programs. Your friend can't understand why the computer industry needs so many different people to do the things that he is doing at home by himself. Explain to your friend why his ideas are wrong.

Case Studies

Part of your course will involve looking at how some systems have been computerised, and the advantages and disadvantages that this may have produced. This is an important part of appreciating computer systems and is called *case studies*.

Case studies are usually left until later in the course so that you have an appreciation of what can and can't be done with computer systems, and can understand the reasons why the hardware and software chosen is like it is, and some of the social implications of installing the system.

We will now consider a very simple case study. However, it will contain all the esstential ingredients of a larger one and show the sort of questions that you could be asked in examinations.

It is essential that you undertake several case studies, not only because it enables you to learn about some applications in detail, but also because there is a large amount of marks on examination papers for doing the chosen case study well.

Example case study

PRESCO SUPERMARKET STORE

PRESCO is an expanding supermarket. Indeed, with the completion of the M25 nearby it is intending to expand into a *hypermarket*.

All the current systems in the supermarket are manually operated. This includes stock control, cash tills, accounts and ordering.

With the intended hypermarket expansion it will not be possible to keep up with the volume of work with the existing work force. Up to 50 checkouts are believed to be necessary. This figure was recommended after a study was carried out by an independent company.

It is intended to install 50 point of sales terminals with laser scanners placed at each checkout. (see page 57 for POS terminals and page 58 for laser scanners.)

At present, to determine if any stock needs ordering the staff go round counting the number of items on each shelf after the supermarket is closed, making a note of the stock level in a pad. At the end of the day, the stock controller looks down the lists to see if any items need ordering. If so, he writes out the order forms and posts them next day to the appropriate suppliers.

An example of a typical order form, filled in for an order placed with Healthy Foods Ltd, is as follows:

```
* * * * * * * * * * * * * * * * * * * * * * * * * * * * * * * * * * * * * * * * * * * * * * * * *
* * * * * * * * * * * * * * * * * * * * * * * * * * * * * * * * * * * * * * * * * * * * * * * * *

                    PRESCO SUPERMARKET LTD.
                          High street
                           Reigate
                            Surrey

    INVOICE NUMBER   000962              DATE   17/3/87

    ACCOUNT NUMBER   PRES 0867/85

    TO:  Healthy Foods Ltd
         Industrial Estate
         Tonbridge
         Kent
    Please supply the following goods to the above address:

         QUANTITY                    ITEM
      1) 300          8 oz    Packets of Muesli Biscuits
      2) 100          16 oz       Packets of Bran Nuts
      3) 50           200g        Chunky Dunky Bars


    Many thanks.
```

The stock controller keeps a carbon copy of each order which is placed in a filing cabinet. When the goods are received he checks them and authorises payment to the appropriate supplier.

It is intended that the computer system should be able to keep stocks at the correct levels, produce the bills for the customers at the POS terminals, produce the invoices to be sent to the suppliers, and work out the profits of the supermarket.

Answers to typical case study

It is usual when dealing with an example case study to write pages of information about how the system was developed and why it was done one way rather than another. However, in your examination you will probably approach case studies by having to answer questions on the likely ways that things have been or could be done. We will therefore pose some questions of the sort that you could get and show the sort of answers that the examiner would be looking for.

What I suggest you do is to *cover up each of the answers* and see if you come up with similar ones. The answers given will certainly not be the only correct ones, but give a very good guide.

QUESTION 1

State *three* advantages that there would be from installing the computerised system.

ANSWERS

1 Fewer errors at the checkout as laser scanners are used to read the bar codes on the products.
2 Ordering is done automatically. Therefore it is unlikely that any item will not be ordered by missing it on the shelf or forgetting to write the invoice out.
3 Much more management information would be available because the computer system could be programmed to give out required information at a moments notice. For example, what goods have not yet been supplied and so on.

QUESTION 2

What sort of computer system do you think would be required by the supermarket?

ANSWER

As there may be a maximum of 50 people using the system at the same time, all requiring a *real time* response then a medium size minicomputer would be necessary. It is vital that there are several hard disc drive units so that the vast amount of information on prices etc. would be instantly available at each of the checkouts.

QUESTION 3

Why is the computer system of stock control better than the manual one?

ANSWER

The manual system requires that staff go round the shelves counting up the stock at the end of each evening. The computer system automatically keeps tabs on what is sold, as it is sold. It is therefore more up to date on placing orders if an item is selling very quickly. Also, people do not have to work late into the evening simply to count up the stock and order the goods for the next day.

QUESTION 4

Give *two* other things that the computer could do to help the business that have not been mentioned already.

ANSWER

1 The computer could work out the payroll for the people in the supermarket. With this information inside the computer, together with other accounts that have to be paid, the computer could easily work out how well the business was doing.
2 The computer could advise the manager on which items were selling very quickly and which items were not. This would give the manager a chance to alter the displays or alter the prices so that slow moving stock could be cleared.

QUESTION 5

What steps would need to be taken by the management of the supermarket to safeguard the business against loss of data in the computer system?

ANSWER

There must be *backup* copies made of all *master* files at regular time intervals. Perhaps at the end of every day when it becomes a hypermarket. These security disks should be kept in a fire-proof safe in a different building to the computer centre at the supermarket.

QUESTION 6

What will be the major difference in the jobs of the cashiers now compared to after the computer has been installed?

ANSWERS

Now: Data is typed in a the keyboard of the cash till by looking at the prices stamped on each of the goods.

After: Many of the items will have bar codes which will be read by the laser scanner. The price will automatically appear on the POS terminal because of the computer. The cashiers will have to learn how to operate the laser scanners and the new POS terminals.

QUESTION 7

Describe the ways in which the stock controller's job will change before and after computerisation.

ANSWER

Before: Lots of paperwork. Working late into the evening to get ordering done. Lots of calculations to be done manually. Typing out of invoices etc.

After: Using a computer keyboard. Hardly any paperwork. Calculations automatically done by computer. No typing of invoices. Automatic printout of stock levels. No late work into the evening. Computer techniques to learn.

QUESTION 8

What extra problems will the introduction of the computer systems pose?

ANSWER

There may be reluctance on the part of some members of staff to change methods with which they are familiar and have been using for years. The computer may go wrong, giving the supermarket a real headache. Therefore, a good maintenance contract will have to be undertaken. Some manual method of operating in a state of emergency may be necessary. For example, forms could be printed so that sales could be carried on in the couple of hours when the computer system was down.